MATTHEW

Spiritual Commentaries on the Bible

New Testament Editor

Mary Ann Getty-Sullivan

Ronald D. Witherup

MATTHEW

God
With Us

New City Press

Published in the United States by New City Press
202 Cardinal Rd., Hyde Park, NY 12538
©2000 Ronald D. Witherup, S.S.

Cover design by Nick Cianfarani

Nihil Obstat: Rev. Paul P. Zilonka, C.P., S.T.D.
Imprimatur: Rev. Msgr. W. Francis Malooly, V.G., Archdiocese of Baltimore

Library of Congress Cataloging-in-Publication Data:

Witherup, Ronald D., 1950-
    Matthew-- God with us / Ronald D. Witherup.
      p. cm.
    ISBN 1-56548-123-2
      1. Bible. N.T. Matthew--Commentaries. I. Title

    BS2575.3 .W55 2000
    226.2'077-dc21   00-041876

1st printing: September 2000
2d printing: January 2002

Printed in Canada

For Jack Dean Kingsbury

Scholar, Teacher, *Doktorvater,* Friend

In honor of his 65th Birthday

Contents

Preface 11

Introduction 13
   The "First" Gospel 13
   Title and Author 14
   Date and Origin 16
   Sources and Gospel Interrelationships 18
   Structure and Content 20
   Historical Background 23
   The Spirituality of Matthew's Gospel 24

I. The Origin and Identity of Jesus Christ, the Son
   of God (1:1–4:16) 28
   The Birth of Jesus (1:18-25) 31
   The Visit of the Magi (2:1-12) 32
   The Massacre of the Innocents and the Return
   to Nazareth (2:13-23) 34
   John the Baptizer (3:1-17) 35
   The Temptation of Jesus in the Desert (4:1-11) 39
   Public Ministry (4:12-17) 41

II. The Preaching and Teaching of Jesus in Galilee
   (4:17–7:29) 43
   Discipleship (4:18-22) 43
   Summary of Jesus' Ministry (4:23-25) 45
   The Sermon on the Mount (5:1–7:28) 47
   The Beatitudes of the Sermon on the Mount (5:1-16) 51
   On Adultery and Divorce (5:27-32) 56
   Oaths, Retaliation, and Love of Enemies (5:33-48) . . 59
   The Our Father (6:1-13) 60

True Riches, Avoiding Judgment, and the Golden
    Rule (6:19-23). 62
The Two Foundations (7:24-29) 64

III. The Healing and Teaching Ministry of Jesus
    (8:1–11:1). 67
Cleansing a Leper (8:1-4) 70
Healing a Centurion's Servant (8:5-13) 71
Peter's Mother-in-Law and Other Miracles
    (8:14-17) 72
The First Digression (8:18-22) 73
Calming a Storm at Sea (8:23-27). 74
Two Miracles and the Second Digression (8:28–9:17) 76
Healing an Official's Daughter, a Woman with
    Hemorrhage and Two Other Miracles (9:18-34) . 79
The Twelve Apostles (10:1-4) 82
Instructions for the Disciples (10:5–11:1). 83

IV. Growing Opposition to Jesus and his Disciples
    (11:2–16:20) 88
John the Baptist (11:2-19). 88
The Impenitent Towns (11:20-24) 91
Praise of the Father and the Gentle Wisdom
    of the Son (11:25-30) 92
Controversy (12:1-21). 93
Further Opposition to Jesus (12:22-45) 96
The True Family of Jesus (12:46-50). 100
The Parable of the Sower and the Seed (13:1-9). . . 101
The Reason for Parables (13:10-17) 104
Jesus at Nazareth (13:54-58). 106
The Death of John the Baptist (14:1-12) 107
Feeding the Five Thousand (14:13-21). 108
Walking on Water, and Summary (14:22-36) 109
Jesus and the Scribes and Pharisees (15:1-20) 111
The Faith of the Canaanite Woman (15:21-28) . . . 113
The Confession of Peter (16:13-20) 115

V. The Ministry of Jesus and the Cost of Discipleship
    (16:21–25:46) 118
    Discipleship and the Cross (16:21-28) 118
    The Transfiguration of Jesus (17:1-13) 120
    Healing of the Possessed Boy and a Second
        Prophecy of the Passion (17:14-23) 122
    The Temple Tax (17:24-27) 124
    Becoming Like a Child (18:1-10) 125
    Parable of the Lost Sheep (18:10-14) 127
    The Life of Community (18:15-35) 128
    Forgiveness (18:21-35) 130
    Marriage, Divorce and Celibacy (19:3-12) 132
    Jesus and the Little Children (19:13-15) 134
    The Rich Young Man (19:16-30) 135
    The Workers in the Vineyard (20:1-16) 138
    Passion-Resurrection Prediction (20:17-28) 140
    The Two Blind Men (20:29-34) 142
    Jesus' Entry into Jerusalem (21:1-11) 143
    Cleansing of the Temple (21:12-17) 145
    The Fig Tree (21:18-22) 146
    Confrontation between Jesus and the Chief
        Priests (21:23-27) 147
    Three Parables (21:28–22:14) 148
    Plotting Against Jesus (22:15-46) 152
    The Hypocrisy of the Scribes and the
        Pharisees (23:1-36) 157
    Lament over Jerusalem (23:37-39) 163
    Destruction and Calamities (24:1-14) 165
    The Great Tribulation (24:15-44) 168
    The Faithful and the Unfaithful Servant (24:45-51) . 172
    The Ten Virgins (25:1-13) 173
    The Talents (25:14-30) 174
    The Parable of the Sheep and Goats (25:31-46) . . . 176

VI. The Passion, Death and Resurrection (26:1–28:20) . . 181
    The Beginning of the Conspiracy (26:1-5) 182
    Anointing of Jesus by a Woman (26:6-13) 183
    The Betrayal (26:14-16) 184

The Last Supper (26:17-35) 185
Agony in the Garden (26:36-56) 188
Arrest and Desertion (26:47-56) 190
The Trial and Judgment (26:57–27:2) 191
Denial (26:69-75) 193
The Fate of Judas (27:3-10) 195
Jesus before Pontius Pilate (27:11-31) 197
The Way of the Cross and the Crucifixion
    (27:32-44) 200
The Death of Jesus (27:45-56) 202
The Burial of Jesus (27:57-66) 205
The Resurrection (28:1-15) 206
The Great Commission (28:16-20) 209

VII. Postscript 211

For Further Study 213

Preface

Commentaries on Matthew's Gospel abound. Many of them, however, are technical in nature and unwieldy for the average Christian to use. In keeping with the aim of this series, the purpose of this commentary is to offer a section-by-section interpretation of Matthew's Gospel in non-technical language to help the reader use this Gospel for personal spiritual enrichment. The perspective is ecumenical, and the scope will include essential insights from the literary, historical and theological perspectives on the Gospel. The nature of such a commentary precludes a detailed treatment of each passage. Yet I have endeavored to offer observations on every section of the Gospel, no matter how briefly.

The translation that accompanies this commentary is the *New American Bible with Revised New Testament* (1986; hereafter NAB). Most, but not all, of the biblical text has been reproduced for easy reference. I will make note of alternative translations only wherever they seem significant for purposes of interpretation. To gain the most from this commentary, always read the actual text of Matthew while studying each part of the Gospel. There is no substitute for your own direct encounter of God's Word. I will often note important cross references whether to the Old Testament (OT) or to other sections of the New Testament (NT). Again I suggest that you read those passages as they arise. They will help you grasp the background of Matthew and broaden your understanding of the spiritual teaching of this Gospel. To assist the reader in meditating on the spiritual message of this Gospel, I will weave into my comments pastoral or spiritual observations that will help the reader apply the text to his or her own life. For best results, I recommend taking the time to sit with the Gospel text and allow it to seep deeply into your consciousness.

Although writing is a solitary task, books are not produced alone. Given the format of this commentary, I cannot pay homage to all those scholars and authors who have contributed to my own understanding of Matthew over the years. I do, however, single out one to whom this book is dedicated. Jack Dean Kingsbury, Aubrey Lee Brooks Professor of Biblical Theology at Union Theological Seminary (Richmond, Virginia), is one of the most influential Matthean scholars of our time. He was the director of my doctoral studies, and I owe him a great debt for all that he taught me. His work has always inspired my love of Matthew's Gospel, and although I may not follow him in every detail, his scholarship has always forced me to think critically about my own interpretations. I also express my profound gratitude to the editors and staff of New City Press for their expert production of this book. Their incredible patience in the face of unexpected delays has made my task of completing the manuscript less daunting. A final word of thanks goes to Mary Ann Getty-Sullivan, editor of this series, for her wise and gentle guidance, and to Paul Zilonka, C.P., who made many helpful comments.

R.D.W.

Introduction

The "First" Gospel

Matthew's Gospel is often known as the First Gospel. This designation is appropriate for several reasons. It is the first book of the NT canon and the first of the four Gospels. Matthew achieved that honored position, in part, because the early Christians thought it had been written by an apostle of Jesus, Matthew the tax collector. This proximity to Jesus justified its status as "first" among the Gospels. In addition, the very content of the Gospel reinforced its premier position. Readers could easily recognize that it is a well-ordered Gospel. Large sections of teaching material dominate it, much of it collected into thematic sections which made it a convenient resource for Christian ethical instruction.

For some nineteen centuries Matthew was the dominant Gospel. It was the most quoted Gospel in the patristic literature. Its version of the Lord's Prayer is the one all Christians recite (despite Luke's version), and children memorize Matthew's Beatitudes (again despite Luke's version). As we shall encounter later in this book, modern biblical scholarship has provided some challenges to this premier status. Most scholars no longer consider Matthew the *earliest* Gospel, nor is the teaching material always the primary focus of the study of Matthew. Yet Matthew continues to wield its considerable influence. We are invited to explore this marvelous Gospel in new and enriching ways. Its time-honored position may have shifted somewhat, but its value, importance and influence on contemporary Christian life remain.

Title and Author

The title of this Gospel—"According to Matthew"—is, like all of the Gospel titles, a second-century A.D. addition. As Christians began to preserve their written traditions in the shape of a "canon," i.e., a collection of authoritative sacred books, titles developed that stemmed from ancient traditions. Christians naturally connected the name Matthew with the account of the tax collector by that name who became one of Jesus' first disciples (Mt 9:9). Matthew, however, was a common name in the first century. Without an identifying surname it would be difficult to pinpoint exactly which Matthew was being referenced. One difficulty of identifying the author of this Gospel with the tax collector is that his name in the parallel accounts (Mk 2:14; Lk 5:27) is "Levi." Some thought of this as a second name or a nickname, but there is no evidence of this practice with two proper names. Scholars have concluded that, like all of the Gospels, Matthew's Gospel was authored by an anonymous second-generation Christian who collected and edited ancient traditions about Jesus of Nazareth into the shape of a Gospel. Throughout this commentary I will use the standard convention of calling this evangelist "Matthew."

Attempting to make more precise the identity of the author remains a challenge. If we cannot name him, can we at least describe some of his background on the basis of the presuppositions in his Gospel? I think we can.

Scholars tend toward two alternatives in identifying Matthew. The predominant theory, and the one I adhere to, is that he was a Jewish-Christian. Various observations support this contention. First, the author was well versed in Jewish traditions. Unlike Mark, Matthew has no need to explain Jewish practices; rather, they are presumed in the background. Second, Matthew is filled with OT quotations and allusions which lend a strongly Jewish flavor to the Gospel. From beginning to end the story of Jesus unfolds under the overarching motif of prophecy and fulfillment. Matthew's unique use of "fulfillment citations" (especially in the infancy narrative and the passion narrative) provides a firm structure for this OT schema. These are often accompanied by the verb "to fulfill" (*pleroun*) and excerpts from a variety of OT passages, especially from the prophets (1:22-23; 2:15,17-18,23; 4:14-16; 8:17; 12:17-21; 13:35; 21:4-5; 27:9-10; cf. 3:3; 13:14-15). Jesus is the fulfillment of Israel's hopes far beyond expectation. Third, contrary to popular conception, Matthew's Jesus does not proclaim a "new law" as much as he teaches and embodies the true interpretation of the Mosaic Law. (Note the absence of the designation "new teaching" found in Mark 1:27.) The Sermon on the Mount itself (ch. 5–7) is not the promulgation of a new law but the redirection and radical application of God's Law revealed to Israel. Matthew's Jesus proclaims: "Do not think that I have come to abolish the law or the prophets. I have come not to abolish but to fulfill" (5:17). Fourth, the use of the peculiar expression "their synagogues" (4:23; 9:35; 10:17) implies that Matthew views his community as somehow related to the synagogue. A breach has occurred between Matthew's community and their Jewish counterparts in a way that paradoxically emphasizes both continuity and newness. Finally, Matthew's ethical perspective seems thoroughly Jewish. The apocalyptic imagery (fire, gnashing of teeth), the emphasis on righteousness as "doing God's will," and the strong use of judgment and damnation themes are all indications of a Jewish outlook.

A minority of scholars thinks of Matthew as a Gentile. They point out that no Jew could make some serious errors regarding Jewish traditions that Matthew seems to make. They draw attention to two pieces of evidence. The first concerns the linkage of the Sadducees with the Pharisees (Mt 16:12; 22:23). In the time of Jesus these Jewish groups were actually bitter enemies. The Sadducees were identified with the Temple in Jerusalem. They were aristocratic rulers who willingly compromised with the Romans. The Pharisees, on the other hand, were a lay group of pious Jews who often opposed the official Temple leadership and who thought of themselves as preserving an authentic Jewish tradition by allowing for oral interpretation of the Torah. How could a Jewish author so confuse the two as to unite them in one designation?

Another problem is the interpretation of the OT. Matthew applies a quotation from the OT to the scene of Jesus' entry into Jerusalem (Mt 21:1-11). The quotation speaks of the king riding "on an ass and on a colt" (Mt 21:5; cf. Zec 9:9 conflated with Is 62:11), and Matthew describes Jesus as sitting "on them" (21:7) as if this were a circus act and Jesus was riding two distinct animals simultaneously. Would a Jewish author read the text as referring to two animals where the common rules of Hebrew poetry would understand such parallelism as a standard expression representing one animal?

I do not believe such problems to be insurmountable. Another approach can be taken as regards the opposition to Jesus. Matthew understands both the Sadducees and Pharisees as united opponents of Jesus. He inelegantly combines these groups (along with scribes and chief priests) into one massive opposition allied with the forces of evil against Jesus. This is merely literary convention, not historical inaccuracy. As for misunderstanding the OT text on occasion, Matthew does not differ widely from common rabbinic interpretational practices which often played with texts in a rather loose manner. At times Jewish interpretation could take texts quite literally where the original sense of the text was more metaphorical or poetic, or vice versa. Matthew's use of the OT can be creative but fits easily within the realm of typical Jewish use of the scriptures.

Date and Origin

Dating and locating the origin of any NT document is usually precarious. Certainty is seldom achievable, and Matthew is no exception. The internal evidence of the Gospel does not provide many clues. The best guess of scholars is that Matthew was written between A.D. 80 and 90, sometime after Mark which was written around A.D. 70. This date seems reasonable, for it coincides with the developing rift that occurred between the synagogue and those Jews who believed that Jesus was the messiah. Matthew reflects the tension between Judaism and Christianity which developed in that period. External evidence provides little help in fixing the date with certainty. Matthew's Gospel was well used in the patristic period. In particular, Ignatius of Antioch (ca. A.D. 35-107) provides the earliest evidence of the use of Matthew and consequently indicates that Matthew circulated before the time of Ignatius. The letters of Ignatius may also provide some evidence that Matthew originated in Syria. Many scholars believe that Matthew reflects an urban environment as compared to Mark's more rural flavor, and Antioch could provide an appropriate urban setting. The second-century tradition of Papias, Bishop of Hierapolis in Asia Minor, witnessed by the Church historian Eusebius (ca. A.D. 260-340), that Matthew was the earliest Gospel and written originally in a Hebrew dialect (Aramaic?), is quite unreliable and based on secondhand information. No evidence exists to support the claim that this Gospel originally existed in some form of Hebrew, although its Jewish flavor is apparent from its perspective and its use of the OT. Matthew's Greek is thoroughly refined, if not the most elegant of the NT. Scholars generally favor that Matthew is secondary to Mark, although a few scholars still argue for Matthew being chronologically the first Gospel.

One might ask: Does it make any difference when and where Matthew was written? I offer a counter question as a response: Can people be better known if you learn something about their background, their heritage, and their upbringing? I think so. I believe having as much background information as possible helps interpreters understand any text better. It can help place Matthew in its proper historical context, flesh out the type of community to whom it was addressed, and provide concrete images of how the Gospel might have been understood by its original hearers. We do not, however, have this information securely, so we need not linger too long over such matters. More important is trying to understand the text itself and its spiritual depth. Where possible, knowledge of first-century history, cultural life, and religious practices can inform our understanding of the text without necessarily providing a resolution to the issues of date and provenance.

Sources and Gospel Interrelationships

The Gospel of Matthew did not appear in a vacuum. The author had sources at his disposal that allowed him to formulate the story of Jesus with some similarity to other such enterprises. Matthew is closely related to Mark and Luke. The three are called the "synoptic Gospels" because they are so similar that they can be laid out in columns side-by-side and studied together. This is the traditional scientific way of studying the Gospels. Since the 19th century this method has led to a preoccupation among scholars to determine what the sources of the Gospels were and who copied from whom. Such close verbal similarity cannot be explained in every case by one source common to all three synoptic Gospels.

The most common theory to explain the complex interrelationship of the synoptics, and the one I assume in this book, is called the "modified two-source hypothesis." According to this theory, Mark is the earliest Gospel. Mark thus provides the basic pattern for both Matthew and Luke. He was the first to collect the parables, teachings, miracle stories, and other "Jesus traditions" and form them into a coherent whole. But scholars have hypothesized the existence of another source document, simply called "Q" (a symbol for the German word for "source"), that consisted primarily of sayings and teachings of Jesus. This document no longer exists, if it ever did. It is a scholarly hypothesis of the material common to Matthew and Luke but not found in Mark. In addition, both Matthew and Luke have other material that is unique to each of them. Thus, two more anonymous and hypothetical sources labeled M and L, respectively, are theorized. The total theory posits two primary sources (Mark and Q) supplemented by two other sources (M for Matthew's special material, and L for Luke's special material). Unfortunately, this theory gets quite complex and leads to all sorts of exaggerated source theories that could disrupt our attempt to mine the Gospel of Matthew for its spiritual riches. I will not dwell on this complexity, but it does impact on how I will read the Gospel.

The most important idea to remember is that, if the two source hypothesis is largely true, then Matthew probably used Mark as his primary source. Matthew, however, did not simply take Mark over wholly. He edited Mark's story as he went along, using at least three different methods:

- *Expansion:* e.g., the addition of an infancy narrative at the beginning (ch. 1–2), long discourses throughout (ch. 5–7;10;18;24–25), and an appearance narrative at the end (ch. 28)

- *Shortening:* e.g., streamlining miracle stories (cf. 9:18-26 with Mk 5:21-43)

- *Other editing by rearrangement, stylistic improvements, and omission:* e.g., leaving out embarrassing details (cf. 12:46-50 with Mk 3:20-21), or changing sequences (cf. 8:1-4 with Mk 1:40-45).

The question of sources is not the most important issue for our purposes. Yet we cannot totally ignore it because it influences the way one reads Matthew. At times it may be helpful to surmise why Matthew changed one aspect or another of Mark's material. Such interpretations, in which the editing process (technically called "redaction") is identified, can provide clues to Matthew's special interests and themes. This method of interpretation, however, will be supplemented with careful literary and narrative interpretations that furnish even more prominent attention to special Matthean interests.

Structure and Content

Another area of ongoing scholarly debate is the structure of the Gospel. No one can dispute that it is a narrative that tells the story of Jesus Christ, the Son of God. Yet the precise structure of this story is open to discussion and disagreement. We will look at three of the most influential proposals before proposing an alternative.

Proposal 1

The most common structure that still appears in many commentaries is based upon a formula that is repeated five times in the Gospel and that concludes five great collections of discourse material (7:28-29; 11:1; 13:53; 19:1; 26:1). The formula (literally translated) is: "And it happened when Jesus had finished . . ." The five collections of teaching supposedly correspond to the five books of Moses (the Pentateuch, the first five books of the OT). Accordingly, the outline of the Gospel is:

1:1–2:23	Prologue	The Birth Narrative
3:1–7:29	Book I	Narrative and sermon
8:1–11:1	Book II	Narrative and discourse on mission
11:2–13:53	Book III	Narrative and teaching on the kingdom
13:54–19:1	Book IV	Narrative and discourse on Church
19:2–26:1	Book V	Narrative and discourse on eschatology
26:2–28:20	Epilogue	The Passion and Resurrection

As attractive and popular as the outline is, it does not do justice to Matthew's Gospel. It overestimates the image of Jesus as a "new Moses" who gives a new law, and it underestimates the role of both the infancy and passion/resurrection narratives, reducing them to mere embellishments to the "teaching" heart of the Gospel. Moreover, there are actually other lengthy discourses in the Gospel besides the main five (cf. 11:7-30; 23:1-39).

20

Proposal 2

Even more complex is a proposal that picks up on the one above which notes the alternation of narrative and discourse material in Matthew. Based upon the generally accepted observation that Matthew is a carefully structured Gospel, some scholars have proposed a *chiastic* outline based upon parallelism. A chiasm is a repeated parallel such as: a,b,c,b',a'. The most popular proposal is:

Sermon	(f) ch. 13 (f')	
Narratives	ch. 11-12 (e)	(e') ch. 14-17
Sermons	ch. 10 (d)	(d') ch. 18
Narratives	ch. 8-9 (c)	(c') ch. 19-22
Sermons	ch. 5-7 (b)	(b') ch. 23-25
Narratives	ch. 1-4 (a)	(a') ch. 26-28

Matthew definitely is attentive to parallelism, repetition and chiasms, a feature of Jewish writings in particular. To make chiasm the main principle of structuring the whole Gospel, however, is untenable. For one thing, the various proposals for chiastic outline of Matthew do not agree on the same chiasms or even the pivotal section of the chiasm. Why would one consider chapter 11 or chapter 13 to be the focus of the Gospel when the action of the Gospel clearly moves toward a climax in the passion and resurrection stories? To make the principle of chiasm the basis for the structure of the whole book is overly ambitious.

Proposal 3

A more recent proposal, supported by those who emphasize the narrative nature of the Gospel, is a simple threefold outline. This approach is based also upon a repeated formula, "From that time on Jesus began to . . ." (4:17 and 16:21, literally translated). The outline yields three parts of a unified story:

I.	1:1–4:16	The Person of Jesus Messiah
II.	4:17–16:20	The Proclamation of Jesus Messiah
III.	16:21–28:20	The Suffering, Death and Resurrection of Jesus Messiah

The advantage of this outline is that it integrates the infancy and passion/resurrection stories into the Gospel, respecting its narrative nature. It also incorporates the five great discourses properly into their narrative context. However, the outline may be just a little too simple to account for some of the other narrative shifts that occur in Matthew.

Proposal 4

Acknowledging the narrative nature of Matthew is important. Matthew tells a story. It meets Aristotle's basic requirement of a narrative—a beginning, a middle and an end. It is populated with characters, plot and a variety of settings. Hence, an alternative narrative outline that I will adopt is as follows:

1:1–4:16	The Origin and Identity of Jesus Christ, the Son of God
4:17–7:29	The Preaching and Teaching of Jesus in Galilee
8:1–11:1	The Healing and Teaching Ministry of Jesus
11:2–16:20	Growing Opposition to Jesus and his Disciples
16:21–25:46	The Ministry of Jesus and the Cost of Discipleship
26:1–28:20	The Passion, Death and Resurrection

I prefer this outline because it takes seriously the narrative flow of Matthew's story of Jesus, incorporates the tracts of teaching material into the plot of the story, and acknowledges other important turning points in the narrative besides the two most obvious ones marked by the formula of 4:17 and 16:21.

There are nearly as many proposed outlines of Matthew's Gospel as there are commentaries. No outline is perfect, yet attempting to understand the outline of a Gospel is helpful in determining its content and interpreting it properly in context.

Understanding the outline of the Gospel and the interrelationships of its various sections helps one to maintain the "big picture." As important as the sections of discourse material are in Matthew, taking seriously the narrative flow of the Gospel will provide us with an approach more appropriate to the nature of the Gospel as literature.

Historical Background

What kind of community is reflected in Matthew's Gospel? What was their life like and what were the daily concerns of its members? Understanding Matthew's Gospel in depth would be easier if we knew precise answers to these questions. Perhaps the experience of developing a friendship provides an analogy. Once you get well acquainted, meet the friend's family, see where that person grew up and what her relatives are like, you begin to know her and understand her better. Unfortunately, knowing the details of Matthew's background is more difficult than meeting the family.

Scholars have made educated guesses that provide a window into the Matthean community. They surmise that Matthew was writing for a mixed community of Jewish and Gentile Christians who lived in an urban environment. The community had at least some rather prosperous members, for Matthew warns against the danger of riches corrupting one's utter devotion to God's kingdom. He also frequently employs various terms for money that indicate a familiarity with wealth (*denarius*, talent, *quadrans*, silver, gold, etc.). The community's relationship to the Jewish community, as noted above, was critical. They were concerned to distinguish themselves from their synagogue counterparts while emphasizing that Jesus and his teaching also provide continuity with the Jewish tradition. This tenuous relationship provided a source of conflict that led to very strong feelings on both parts, as witnessed by the vitriol of chapter 23. This external tension was also exacerbated by internal dissension. Matthew's community had some anxiety about members who did not live up to the community's high moral expectations. Church discipline was an issue (Mt 18:15-20), yet Jesus' message of reconciliation and forgiveness provided a means of handling such delicate matters. The evangelist also emphasizes that God is the one who will bring judgment. Consequently, he urges a restrained attitude towards members of the community who are bad influences. The weeds are allowed to grow with the wheat until the day of judgment (13:24-30).

Since scholars have not been able to agree exactly where Matthew's Gospel originated, we cannot say for certain what were the historical circumstances that shaped the Gospel. Traditional methods of interpretation often emphasized that the text was a *window* through which one could view the Matthean community. Such an approach has a certain validity, but it does not provide absolute certainty and it can over-emphasize the historical issues to the detriment of theological ones. This commentary will utilize this traditional approach while incorporating techniques that view the text as a *mirror* in which we see ourselves and our own situation reflected. The combination, I think, will prove fruitful.

The Spirituality of Matthew's Gospel

Christians read the Gospels primarily because they want to be inspired somehow by God's Word. How does Matthew inspire? This section aims to provide a simple road map to guide you in your exploration of Matthew. Matthew, I believe, has its own spirituality or spiritual teaching that can be briefly summarized to point the way to fruitful interpretation.

Two major themes intersect deep in the heart of Matthew's Gospel—Christology and ecclesiology. Christologically, Matthew is most concerned to tell the story of the messiah and God's Son, Jesus of Nazareth, as he has come to know it. To this end, he employs a variety of christological titles throughout the Gospel (Son of God, Son of Man, Son of David, Lord, Christ, Emmanuel, etc.), and he tells the story with great reverence.

24

Even the name "Jesus" is christological, for Matthew points out its meaning (1:21) and uses it with far greater frequency than the other Gospels (150 times compared to Mark's 81 and Luke's 89). He aims to instruct his audience about the origin, identity, mission, and religious significance of Jesus Christ. He interweaves with this primary story the opposition that Jesus faced. God has enemies, Satan and all his allied forces of evil. As God's Son, Jesus bears the brunt of this opposition. As Jesus' story unfolds, so does the opposition he encounters. It is a story of cosmic proportions in which good and evil clash head-on.

But another major theme intersects with this story line. Ecclesiologically, Matthew is concerned to describe the nature of the Church as he has come to know it. Matthew, in fact, is often called "the Gospel of the Church" because it is the only Gospel to mention the word "Church" (*ekklesia*; 16:18; 18:17). This theme centers on the disciples of Jesus. They constitute a new community whose lives are forever changed because of their association with Jesus Christ. Much of Matthew's teaching material focuses on explicit or implicit instruction to the disciples. In this fashion Matthew sets forth his under-standing of the Church as the group that follows Jesus on the path of righteousness. The Church is a new people, a new family, whose duty is to evangelize the world.

These two themes, then, direct in large part the spiritual teaching of Matthew. As we engage the Gospel, we should be on the lookout for Matthew's understanding of Jesus Christ and of the Church (the disciples). Intermingled throughout the Gospel are many other thematic clues to Matthew's spiritual interests. I list twelve of them here:

- *Prophecy and fulfillment:* God's plan was foretold by the prophets and finds its fulfillment in Jesus;

- *God's relationship to Jesus:* God is a loving Father whose primary desire is for mercy, not sacrifices; Jesus is the

25

faithful and obedient Son (Matthew calls God Father some 40 times as compared to Mark's 2 times.);

- *Emmanuel*: Jesus is God-with-us who abides with his people forever even down to the tiniest remnant of faithful ones;

- *Jesus the messiah*: Jesus has the power in word and deed to heal people and bring them salvation;

- *Universalism*: Jesus brings salvation to all, including the Gentiles;

- *Righteousness*: God desires humans to live ethically upright lives for which they will be held accountable;

- *Final judgment*: a time of separation of good and bad, accompanied by much apocalyptic imagery about fire, weeping, gnashing of teeth;

- *Discipleship*: following Jesus is not easy, and it will involve humility, suffering and rejection; it means a share in Jesus' ministry;

- *Faith and doubt*: believing in Jesus often is accompanied by questions or doubts, but fear is the real enemy of faith;

- *Conversion*: encountering Jesus requires acknowledging one's sinfulness, accepting God's forgiveness, and extending forgiveness to others;

- *Prayer*: prayer should be simple, regular, humble, and heartfelt;

- *Evangelization*: Jesus sends his disciples into the world to baptize and make disciples, proclaiming the gospel message.

This list is by no means comprehensive. Many other themes and motifs exist in the Gospel to which I will draw attention in the commentary. Yet one can obtain here a broad orientation to the breadth of Matthew's spiritual teaching. I should emphasize that much of Matthew is geared toward Christian ethics. Matthew is the evangelist most concerned about ethical behavior and its consequences. Thus, there are many moralistic teachings in the Gospel. One must try to balance this perspective with awareness of other themes, but one would not exaggerate to say that Matthew's spirituality has many ethical overtones to it. For Matthew, holiness cannot be separated from how we live our lives day to day confronting the ethical decisions that we encounter. His is a "maximalist" spirituality. It calls forth the very best of the human spirit in light of God's graciousness. Matthew's words are as rich today in spiritual depth as they ever were in the first century. Our challenge is to try to understand what he has to say and how to apply it to our own lives as we confront the third Christian millennium.

I

The Origin and Identity of Jesus Christ, the Son of God

(1:1–4:16)

Unlike Mark, who jumps right into the story of Jesus by introducing John the Baptist as Jesus' forerunner, Matthew takes a more temperate approach at the beginning of his Gospel. Matthew prefers to set forth the background of his protagonist in a more careful and structured manner. The very first line of the Gospel provides significant clues for understanding Jesus. Matthew presents his "book of the genealogy" of Jesus who is the messiah, the Christ. This line serves double duty. It begins the genealogical list that establishes Jesus' family history, but it also begins the entire "book" of Matthew. The use of the Greek word *genesis* for genealogy may evoke other allusions. It also means "origin" and "beginning" and recalls the name of the first book of the OT. Matthew thus alludes to a new beginning with Jesus. In Jesus the messiah, God begins a new act of salvation, one that will establish a new people in a new kind of relationship with God and with one another. The new and the old combine in Jesus in an act of fulfillment.

Two other designations are important for understanding Jesus at the outset of Matthew's story. He is simultaneously "son of David" and "son of Abraham." The first clearly establishes him in line with Israel's most famous king and most important royal lineage. That Jesus is Davidic in background guarantees that he has the right credentials to fulfill Israel's hope for a messiah. In first century Judaism messianic expectations among Jews had largely centered on the Davidic line. Matthew reminds the readers throughout his story about Jesus'

28

Davidic lineage, especially through the repeated title "son of David" (1:20; 9:27; 12:23; 15:22; 20:30,31; 21:9,15). Being "son of Abraham" is a little more subtle. Abraham, of course, was a Gentile who became Israel's father of faith (Gn 12:1-7). More important was God's promise to Abraham that he would become the father of the nations of the earth (Gn 12:3; 13:16; 18:18), a picture of a universal family all united in God's love. Matthew views Jesus as the fulfillment of this vision. In Jesus, son of Abraham, all will be welcomed into God's kingdom. Paradoxically, this thoroughly Jewish messiah of thoroughly Jewish background will be the means of bringing the Gentiles into God's kingdom (8:10-12; 28:19), bringing to full circle the promise God made to Abraham. This image contains the seeds of a modern hope for unity in the human family, for three of the world's main religions—Judaism, Islam, and Christianity—all claim Abraham as their founding ancestor of faith. The Christian claim that Jesus is a universal Savior for all people is, for Matthew, no exaggeration but a fulfillment of God's plan.

The genealogy itself is a stumbling block for some modern readers. It seems a boring bit of antiquated history. (It is one passage I chose not to reproduce.) This may have been noticed more in older translations that used the verb "begat" at each interval in the list. But this reaction is curious given recent modern interest in family genealogies. Americans, in particular, have become more sensitized to family histories. Computer programs now exist that allow people to create their own family tree. Fleshing out this history helps us understand our own origins. Matthew attempts a similar enterprise with Jesus' genealogy. If Matthew, however, was trying to write a history, we would have to judge him poorly. The list is obviously artificially constructed. Not only is there the arbitrary structure of three sets of fourteen generations leading up to the messiah, but also the names of many kings are left off the list. Is Matthew writing an abridged history of Israel's royalty? No, for his interests are more theological than historical.

Three observations will help us explore this genealogy. First, Abraham and David are the keys to the list. They appear at the beginning and end of the list (1:1,17) and reinforce why Jesus is *son* of both of them. Second, the traditional male list is broken up in five places by women—Tamar, Rahab, Ruth, Bathsheba (=wife of Uriah) and Mary. The first four all have tainted reputations in some fashion. Either they are foreigners, non-Jews, or they have a problematic sexual history. Drawing attention to "the wife of Uriah" (Mt 1:6) heightens the remembrance that David not only committed adultery with Bathsheba, but he had her husband murdered as well. The Davidic lineage, in other words, is not pristine. The reference to Mary also fits this pattern. A woman will be the bearer of the messiah under strange and miraculous circumstances. The phrase, "of her was born Jesus" breaks the traditional genealogical formula ("became the father of") and alludes to the miraculous conception and birth that is about to take place. The upshot of all this becomes clear. In the messianic lineage, there is both continuity and discontinuity with Israel's history. God's will can be accomplished even with less than perfect human instruments. A tiny thread of wickedness runs through the tapestry of Israel's history, but it will not prevent God's promise of a messiah from coming to fruition. This is not a green light to sin, but a simple reminder that God works in mysterious ways that defy human convention.

A third comment is that the number fourteen is also artificial. Ancient Jewish writers had a fondness for numbers. They could hold great symbolic value. Matthew's use of fourteen may reflect the numerical value of the name David in its Hebrew characters. It could be subtle way of supporting the importance of the Davidic line. Yet how does one explain the presence of only thirteen kings in the last of the three divisions? Matthew is telling us that the fulfillment of the Davidic line in Jesus has come to its last and greatest hope. The cycle will not continue, for he is the apex of the development.

The Birth of Jesus (1:18-25)

[18] Now this is how the birth of Jesus Christ came about. When his mother Mary was betrothed to Joseph, but before they lived together, she was found with child through the holy Spirit. [19] Joseph her husband, since he was a righteous man, yet unwilling to expose her to shame, decided to divorce her quietly. [20] Such was his intention when, behold, the angel of the Lord appeared to him in a dream and said, "Joseph, son of David, do not be afraid to take Mary your wife into your home. For it is through the holy Spirit that this child has been conceived in her. [21] She will bear a son and you are to name him Jesus, because he will save his people from their sins." [22] All this took place to fulfill what the Lord had said through the prophet:

[23] "Behold, the virgin shall be with child
and bear a son,
and they shall name him Emmanuel,"

which means "God is with us." [24] When Joseph awoke, he did as the angel of the Lord had commanded him and took his wife into his home. [25] He had no relations with her until she bore a son, and he named him Jesus.

The genealogy leads directly to the conception and birth of Jesus. The dreams that guide the process are symbolic that God is directing the events, not the human characters. Dreams were considered direct messages from God. Joseph, like his OT namesake who was also a dreamer (Gn 40–41), is guided at every step in the process by divine intervention. In a dream an angel tells him how to name the child with two designations that will bear significance for the rest of the Gospel. Jesus (Hebrew *Yeshua*) means "Yahweh saves," and Jesus' mission will be to save his people from their sins (1:21), words that will be remembered at the Last Supper (26:28). Only Matthew exalts Jesus' name in this fashion and invokes it with regularity (around 150 times). The other name, Emmanuel (God with us) forms an overarching theme in the Gospel. It comes from the prophet Isaiah who originally spoke the words of hope to King Ahaz in troubled times (Is 7:14). God's nearness to people, especially the chosen people, is assured in the presence of Jesus. Whether it happens when only two or three are together (18:20) or as a promise for all ages (28:20), Jesus is God-with-us. For a Jewish-Christian audience these words may have held particular value. Traditionally, the Jews held that God's presence was centered in the Temple in Jerusalem. After the destruction of Jerusalem in AD 70, they could no longer rely on that presence. God had to be found in other ways, such as in the Torah or synagogue ceremonies. Matthew's community, however, could now look to Jesus as the new locus for God's acts of salvation. His presence in word and deed would become a hallmark of this community and of Christians for all time.

The Visit of the Magi (2:1-12)

[1] When Jesus was born in Bethlehem of Judea, in the days of King Herod, behold, magi from the east arrived in Jerusalem, [2] saying, "Where is the newborn king of the Jews? We saw his star at its rising and have come to do him homage." [3] When King Herod heard this, he was greatly troubled, and all Jerusalem with him. [4] Assembling all the chief priests and the scribes of the people, he inquired of them where the Messiah was to be born. [5] They said to him, "In Bethlehem of Judea, for thus it has been written through the prophet:
[6] 'And you, Bethlehem, land of Judah,
    are by no means least among the rulers of Judah;
    since from you shall come a ruler,
    who is to shepherd my people Israel.' "
[7] Then Herod called the magi secretly and ascertained from them the time of the star's appearance. [8] He sent them to Bethlehem and said, "Go and search diligently for the child. When you have found him, bring me word, that I too may go and do him homage." [9] After their audience with the king they set out. And behold, the star that they had seen at its rising preceded them, until it came and stopped over the place

where the child was. [10]They were overjoyed at seeing the star, [11]and on entering the house they saw the child with Mary his mother. They prostrated themselves and did him homage. Then they opened their treasures and offered him gifts of gold, frankincense, and myrrh. [12]And having been warned in a dream not to return to Herod, they departed for their country by another way.

This scene, the visit of the magi, is also unique to Matthew. Our images are influenced incurably by countless Christmas creche scenes of three wise men on camels bearing gifts for a new-born infant. Later tradition even gave them names—Caspar, Balthasar and Melchior. But Matthew is not interested in such intricate details. What concerns Matthew is the contrast between the Jewish leaders and these strange foreign figures from afar. Herod was troubled, "and all Jerusalem with him" (2:3) when the magi arrive seeking a new-born "king." Herod even consults the chief priests and scribes, the leaders who should know from their scriptures about the birth of the messiah. They correctly cite a passage about Bethlehem (Mi 5:1), but they do not understand its significance. Nor does Herod understand the nature of this new "king." While Herod seeks to destroy the child, the magi follow God's miraculous sign (the star) and worship the child. Paying Jesus homage reflects their proper attitude of faith (vv. 2,11 *proskyneo*, cf. 9:18; 14:33; 28:9,17). In this short scene Matthew has given us an ironic motif. Those who should be "insiders" remain blind in their obtuseness to God's will, while "outsiders" properly follow God's clues and are enlightened in the process. Matthew will be unremitting in his estimation that the Jewish leadership, from the birth to the death of Jesus, failed to heed God's messages to them. They had every advantage (Jewish heritage, the Torah, the prophets), but they resisted, while outsiders read the "signs of the times" better. Matthew's perspective gives us fair warning. There are two ways of responding to God's presence; we should not presume that we will necessarily choose correctly. The magi thus represent the Gentiles who came into the Christian community once many Jews had rejected the message of Jesus. Later I will address the delicate issue of how this seemingly anti-Jewish sentiment in Matthew had horrendous consequences in history.

The Massacre of the Innocents and the Return to Nazareth (2:13-23)

[13] When they had departed, behold, the angel of the Lord appeared to Joseph in a dream and said, "Rise, take the child and his mother, flee to Egypt, and stay there until I tell you. Herod is going to search for the child to destroy him." [14] Joseph rose and took the child and his mother by night and departed for Egypt. [15] He stayed there until the death of Herod, that what the Lord had said through the prophet might be fulfilled, "Out of Egypt I called my son."

[16] When Herod realized that he had been deceived by the magi, he became furious. He ordered the massacre of all the boys in Bethlehem and its vicinity two years old and under, in accordance with the time he had ascertained from the magi. [17] Then was fulfilled what had been said through Jeremiah the prophet:

[18] "A voice was heard in Ramah,
   sobbing and loud lamentation;
Rachel weeping for her children,
   and she would not be consoled,
   since they were no more."

[19] When Herod had died, behold, the angel of the Lord appeared in a dream to Joseph in Egypt [20] and said, "Rise, take the child and his mother and go to the land of Israel, for those who sought the child's life are dead." [21] He rose, took the child and his mother, and went to the land of Israel. [22] But when he heard that Archelaus was ruling over Judea in place of his father Herod, he was afraid to go back there. And because he had been warned in a dream, he departed for the region of Galilee. [23] He went and dwelt in a town called Nazareth, so

that what had been spoken through the prophets might be fulfilled, "He shall be called a Nazorean."

The rejection motif does not stop there. Herod relentlessly pursues the child by murdering innocent male infants in Bethlehem in a desperate bid to destroy a perceived rival. Again Matthew applies an OT word from Jeremiah to explain that this tragedy reflects prophetic experience (Jer 31:15). But Herod's plan is thwarted once more by Joseph the dreamer who is told to flee with the child and its mother to Egypt. We should notice that up until now the child has never been named again in the narrative. Lingering in the background are the names Jesus and Emmanuel, but the focus has been only on "the child." Matthew now reveals the reason for not repeating the name. The flight into Egypt and the subsequent residence at Nazareth happened so that prophetic words could be fulfilled once more. Like Israel of old but in a far superior manner, he is the "son" called out of Egypt (Hos 11:1). And he will be known as a "Nazorean," probably an allusion to someone devoted to God (Jgs 13:5-7) and of messianic destiny (Is 11:1). At every step along the path, Jesus' life and ministry will be at the service of his heavenly Father and the sacred scriptures. He is the fulfillment of Israel's hopes, enunciated with clarity in the prophetic Word of God. The reader is thus drawn into the identity of this obedient and faithful son whose death will bring life to a new people.

John the Baptizer (3:1-17)

[1] In those days John the Baptist appeared, preaching in the desert of Judea [2] [and] saying, "Repent, for the kingdom of heaven is at hand!" [3] It was of him that the prophet Isaiah had spoken when he said:

"A voice of one crying out in the desert,
'Prepare the way of the Lord,
make straight his paths.'"

⁴John wore clothing made of camel's hair and had a leather belt around his waist. His food was locusts and wild honey. ⁵ At that time Jerusalem, all Judea, and the whole region around the Jordan were going out to him ⁶ and were being baptized by him in the Jordan River as they acknowledged their sins.

⁷ When he saw many of the Pharisees and Sadducees coming to his baptism, he said to them, "You brood of vipers! Who warned you to flee from the coming wrath? ⁸ Produce good fruit as evidence of your repentance. ⁹ And do not presume to say to yourselves, 'We have Abraham as our father.' For I tell you, God can raise up children to Abraham from these stones.¹⁰ Even now the ax lies at the root of the trees. Therefore every tree that does not bear good fruit will be cut down and thrown into the fire. ¹¹ I am baptizing you with water, for repentance, but the one who is coming after me is mightier than I. I am not worthy to carry his sandals. He will baptize you with the holy Spirit and fire. ¹² His winnowing fan is in his hand. He will clear his threshing floor and gather his wheat into his barn, but the chaff he will burn with unquenchable fire."

The tone of the story now shifts with the appearance of John the Baptist. Suddenly years have passed and we are brought into the presence of a rather strange prophetic figure whose message will precede the exact same message as Jesus (cf. 3:2; 4:17). He, too, is said to fulfill prophetic words, in this case, those of Isaiah. John is a voice that cries out in the desert, one who prepares the way for another (3:3). To make it absolutely clear that John's identity is bound to Elijah, who was expected to return prior to the appearance of the messiah, Matthew paints him in prophetic hues with strange garments and a vegetarian diet (cf. 3:4; 2 Kgs 1:8). Jesus will later confirm that John is Elijah (11:7-14), but for now what is essential is John's message. God's kingdom is breaking into the world, but it must be accompanied by repentance for sins. John proceeds to describe in vivid terms that judgment awaits those who refuse the baptism of repentance. Using stock apocalyptic imagery, John's message is to produce "good fruit" (=righteous life) or risk being cut down and thrown into the fire (=the punishment of Gehenna or hell).

We cannot shrink from Matthew's portrait of John. He is a stern preacher, an untiring voice for repentance. He warns that we cannot rely on heritage alone (3:9, "Abraham as our father"). Rather, conformity to God's kingdom involves putting into one's life what God requires of us. John's message is a clarion call of one aspect of Jesus' message, but it does not embrace it all. Whereas his baptism is with water, Jesus will baptize "with the holy Spirit and fire" (3:11). And whereas John urges us to "get your act together," Jesus will also insist that forgiveness of one another's failings must accompany the urgent call to transform our lives (18:21-22). We should not exaggerate their differences. Both proclaim the message of repentance, both warn of impending judgment, both condemn the Jewish leadership, and both suffer martyrdom. John is Jesus' forerunner in multiple ways. John's message prepares for the more powerful messenger.

[13] Then Jesus came from Galilee to John at the Jordan to be baptized by him. [14] John tried to prevent him, saying, "I need to be baptized by you, and yet you are coming to me?" [15] Jesus said to him in reply, "Allow it now, for thus it is fitting for us to fulfill all righteousness." Then he allowed him. [16] After Jesus was baptized, he came up from the water and behold, the heavens were opened [for him], and he saw the Spirit of God descending like a dove [and] coming upon him. [17] And a voice came from the heavens, saying, "This is my beloved Son, with whom I am well pleased."

The next scene brings John and Jesus on the same stage for a dramatic moment. Jesus' baptism makes clear the relationship between John and Jesus in Matthew's eyes. John recognizes that he is the inferior party who should yield to the superior, but

Jesus insists that his own baptism be accomplished "to fulfill all righteousness" (3:15). Righteousness (*dikaiosyne*) is an important Matthean theme with Jewish background. Righteousness is basically a right relationship with God. It involves morally and ethically living out God's law in daily life. When the OT calls people to "walk in the ways of the Lord," it is the call to righteousness. How does Jesus fulfill all righteousness? For Matthew, Jesus does this in word and deed. In word, especially the Sermon on the Mount (ch. 5–7), he shows that he both understands and interprets God's law correctly. He knows the difference between essentials and accidentals. Indeed, his many miracles (e.g., ch. 8–9) show that he has God's power to accomplish what is humanly impossible. He allows himself to be baptized, then, to initiate his mission in word and deed to proclaim his heavenly father's message. It becomes a most dramatic moment of his identity revealed for all to see. The Spirit anoints him and a heavenly voice confirms: "This is my beloved Son, with whom I am well pleased" (3:17). The revelatory moment arrives to confirm his origins and identity, which up till now have been understood only by the readers rather than by the characters in the story. Jesus is God's Son. That is why he will be able to save his people and will surpass even John the Baptist in greatness.

The fact of Jesus' baptism was a scandal to the early Church. The short dialogue between John and Jesus shows that Matthew's community may have been troubled by Jesus' baptism, for they had already come to associate baptism with forgiveness of sins. How could God's Son need baptism? Matthew addresses that question by showing that Jesus' baptism had two purposes. It revealed his origins and identity, and it empowered him in the Spirit to defeat evil. The issue of sinfulness thus recedes in the background. Most important is keeping our eyes on Jesus in word and in deed. Another feature of Jesus' baptism for us to keep in mind is the notion of surrender to God's will. Matthew's community obviously practiced baptism as a means of entry into the community (28:19).

Baptism can be an empowerment for ministry. We must place ourselves at God's disposal in order to receive the strength necessary to combat evil. Doing righteous deeds is not easy. It requires enormous spiritual strength, especially in the face of social pressures. Baptism begins to give us that strength.

The Temptation of Jesus in the Desert (4:1-11)

[1] Then Jesus was led by the Spirit into the desert to be tempted by the devil. [2] He fasted for forty days and forty nights, and afterwards he was hungry. [3] The tempter approached and said to him, "If you are the Son of God, command that these stones become loaves of bread." [4] He said in reply, "It is written:

'One does not live by bread alone,
but by every word that comes forth from the mouth of God.'"

[5] Then the devil took him to the holy city, and made him stand on the parapet of the temple, [6] and said to him, "If you are the Son of God, throw yourself down. For it is written:

'He will command his angels concerning you'
and 'with their hands they will support you,
lest you dash your foot against a stone.'"

[7] Jesus answered him, "Again it is written, 'You shall not put the Lord, your God, to the test.'" [8] Then the devil took him up to a very high mountain, and showed him all the kingdoms of the world in their magnificence, [9] and he said to him, "All these I shall give to you, if you will prostrate yourself and worship me." [10] At this, Jesus said to him, "Get away, Satan! It is written:

'The Lord, your God, shall you worship
and him alone shall you serve.'"

[11] Then the devil left him and, behold, angels came and ministered to him.

Following the baptism the Spirit leads Jesus out into the desert. The desert, we might remember, is the locale of demons and temptation. Israel had been sorely tested in the desert (Exodus and Numbers), John the Baptist's preaching took place in the desert, and Jesus is led to the desert to confront evil face to face. It is a spiritual test accompanied by fasting and prayer. It lasts the biblically symbolic forty days and nights, indicating a lengthy time reminiscent of Moses' time of fasting and prayer with the Lord (see Ex 24:18; 34:28).

One thing about a spiritual test is that the devil is never far away. If God's Spirit drove Jesus to the test, the tempter seizes the opportunity. The spiritual test is not any old test, nor is it a series of trivial temptations. On the contrary, the tempter aims for the Achilles heel! "If you are the Son of God ..." (4:3,6)—these words challenge Jesus' identity to his core. His sonship is what is at stake. Is he truly worthy, are his "credentials" sufficient to withstand the temptations that come his way? In each of the three temptations, quotations from the Book of Deuteronomy are used. It's a little bit like biblical jeopardy. Who can quote the best scripture passage? The temptations appear to be in ascending order. The most mundane comes first (hunger, bread), followed by health (dashing against rocks), and finally power (kingdoms of the world). In each case Jesus responds with a scriptural teaching that indicates he cannot be tricked to use his identity for his own welfare. The Deuteronomic passages, however, hold deeper significance. Israel of old succumbed to temptation periodically despite God's provision of manna, water, and sustenance in the desert. Where they failed, Jesus will succeed. Satan is a powerful adversary who will return often in the Gospel in the form of demons (8:16,28; 9:32 etc.), but he will never damage the armor of Jesus' Sonship. Jesus proves himself the obedient and faithful Son precisely in his unwillingness to use his status on his own behalf, even when the temptation returns at its most critical time (27:39-43).

Another important detail is that the final temptation takes place on "a very high mountain" (4:8). Mountains were thought to be the dwelling place of the gods. In the biblical tradition the mountain is also a place of revelation (1 Kgs 19:8), where God and Moses had communed (Ex 19:3,20), where the Torah had been given (Ex 20), where sacrifices were to be made (1 Kgs 18:19,38), and where worship was centered (Mount Zion, Is 4:3). Key moments in Jesus' life, according to Matthew, take place on mountains, symbolic of his closeness to God. In addition to the final temptation in this scene, Jesus gives his first major sermon on a mountain (5:1; 8:1), heals on a mountain (15:29), is transfigured and has his identity confirmed on a mountain (17:1), and appears to his disciples on a mountain to instruct them on their mission (28:16). In short, the mountain is a place where Jesus is much at home, not to escape the trials and tribulations of life but to be immersed in them in a deeper and more challenging way.

Public Ministry (4:12-17)

[12] When he heard that John had been arrested, he withdrew to Galilee. [13] He left Nazareth and went to live in Capernaum by the sea, in the region of Zebulun and Naphtali, [14] that what had been said through Isaiah the prophet might be fulfilled:
[15] "Land of Zebulun and land of Naphtali,
the way to the sea, beyond the Jordan,
Galilee of the Gentiles,
[16] the people who sit in darkness
have seen a great light,
on those dwelling in a land overshadowed by death
light has arisen."
[17] From that time on, Jesus began to preach and say, "Repent, for the kingdom of heaven is at hand."

The final section of this first major division of Matthew describes the beginning of Jesus' public ministry (4:12-17). Only after John the Baptist is arrested can Jesus' ministry begin. Jesus' message, like John's, concerns conversion and the arrival of God's kingdom ("kingdom of heaven"). For Matthew, the kingdom is not simply a place but God's rule or reign over the universe. In Jesus, God has come near spatially and temporally to God's people. He is God's presence in their midst who has begun the eschatological fulfillment God had promised. Like the infancy story, this act is also overshadowed by the fulfillment of scripture. Jesus moves from Nazareth to Capernaum to fulfill an Isaian vision about Galilee (Is 9:1-2). Matthew quotes some form of the passage not found in either the Hebrew Bible (the Jewish scriptures, our OT) or the Septuagint (the Greek translation of the OT). His primary interest, however, is on the image of "Galilee of the Gentiles" (4:15). Jesus' ministry will paradoxically find more success among the Gentiles than among his own kindred Jews. The Gentiles are described as a people sitting in darkness who need the light to shine on them. Jesus is that light. At the cross, guarded by Gentile soldiers, that light will finally shine on them and they will acknowledge him clearly as God's Son (27:54). When Jesus *begins* (4:17) his mission, armed with the Spirit's power and John's message of repentance on his lips, we already have been given clues as to where it will lead. Just as Herod had acted against Jesus and the magi had accepted him, so others throughout the Gospel will prove themselves to be on one side or the other. Faith ultimately requires a decision. Matthew will not have us shirk that responsibility.

II

The Preaching and Teaching
of Jesus in Galilee
(4:17–7:29)

Discipleship (4:18-22)

[18] As he was walking by the Sea of Galilee, he saw two brothers, Simon who is called Peter, and his brother Andrew, casting a net into the sea; they were fishermen. [19] He said to them, "Come after me, and I will make you fishers of men." [20] At once they left their nets and followed him. [21] He walked along from there and saw two other brothers, James, the son of Zebedee, and his brother John. They were in a boat, with their father Zebedee, mending their nets. He called them, [22] and immediately they left their boat and their father and followed him.

The first action in Jesus' ministry after announcing the main theme of the nearness of God's kingdom is to call his first disciples (4:18-22). Jesus is not a lone ranger. Although he possesses a unique identity and destiny, Jesus invites others to share his mission. The prophetic word of an extended outreach to the Gentiles that had introduced Jesus' own message (4:15-16) will require an extended family to carry it beyond Israel's boundaries. So Matthew consistently shows us that Jesus includes others in his mission. But look whom Jesus calls—common fishermen, not the religious elite that one might expect for a religious mission. The first group consists of two sets of brothers, Simon and Andrew, and James and John, the sons of Zebedee. Three of them will form an inner circle—Simon, James, John (cf. 17:1; 26:37)—among the twelve who will eventually be called and designated *apostles* (10:2, the only occurrence of the word in Matthew). The twelve will assist with judging the tribes of Israel (19:28). Significantly, they do not seek Jesus. Rather, he sees them doing their traditional work, fishing, and immediately issues the call to discipleship with the simple invitation: "Come after me."

Jesus' simple words constitute the invitation to discipleship that endures in every age. Others besides the twelve hear the same invitation (e.g., the rich young man in 19:21). Indeed, this is the call issued to us in our own day; the only question is whether we hear it and respond appropriately. The response of these first disciples provides a model for all others, for it is unquestioning and immediate. The text uses the technical term for discipleship in saying that they "followed" him (*ekolouthesan;* cf. 8:19,22; 9:9; 10:38; 16:24; 19:21,27,28), even to the point of James and John abandoning their father who was in the boat with them. They all abandon their nets, but they will still be fishing, for Jesus says that he will make them "fishers of men" (4:19). They will be casting a different kind of net by their own preaching and healing, and they abandon one kind of boat and one kind of family for new ones. The new boat will be a church (see 8:23; 16:18), and the new family will be a family of disciples who have only one father, their heavenly Father (see 12:50). In one very simple passage, Matthew has illustrated several aspects of the impact of Jesus' ministry. A whole new group of faithful will be formed. Beginning in "Galilee of the Gentiles" they will eventually go forth to a worldwide ministry gathering in those who will hear and accept the message of repentance and the nearness of God's kingdom (28:19-20).

Even such a simple scene can instruct us spiritually. Three elements come to the fore regarding discipleship. First, Jesus initiates the call. We might be seekers and might well be "gung ho" to do God's will, but ultimately we must ask whether we have been listening carefully enough to hear the call that God issues. Second, Jesus calls his disciples from where they are at in the midst of their ordinary, daily lives. There is no special setting, no exceptional preparation. What is demanded, however, is an immediate and unquestioning response. That can be one of the most difficult aspects of discipleship, but the third element is even more challenging. Jesus's call leads to an abandonment of all that is familiar: job, environment, and even family. The cost of discipleship, as Dietrich Bonhoeffer once wrote about in his famous book of that title, is great. Later, Jesus promises that those who make this sacrifice will be rewarded (19:29), but that does not ameliorate the sacrifice that must be made. Discipleship entails risk, as Matthew's story of Jesus will demonstrate when even some of the inner circle will prove themselves lacking in the faith necessary to sustain all the trials and tribulations discipleship can bring.

Summary of Jesus' Ministry (4:23-25)

> [23] He went around all of Galilee, teaching in their synagogues, proclaiming the gospel of the kingdom, and curing every disease and illness among the people. [24] His fame spread to all of Syria, and they brought to him all who were sick with various diseases and racked with pain, those who were possessed, lunatics, and paralytics, and he cured them. [25] And great crowds from Galilee, the Decapolis, Jerusalem, and Judea, and from beyond the Jordan followed him.

The following scene is what is called a "summary scene." Matthew collapses time into a short passage that summarizes what Jesus was doing in the days following his call of the first disciples (4:23-25). In typically balanced fashion, Matthew parallels it with another summary scene in which time is similarly telescoped into a summation of Jesus' ministry (9:35-38). Note that the language is virtually the same in two verses (cf. 4:23 and 9:35). The parallel suggests that readers are to see these passages as bookends that tie everything in between together in some fashion. In fact, chapters 5–9 can be seen as a package with two compartments. The first compartment that encompasses the great Sermon on the Mount shows Jesus as the messiah in word (ch. 5–7). The second compartment that describes Jesus' ministry of healing, which itself is the focus of each of the summary passages, shows Jesus to be the messiah in deed (ch. 8–9). Both his words and actions confirm his identity revealed in the infancy narrative and reiterated in the baptism. Were he not God's Son, he could not effectively preach, teach and heal as he does. His "gospel of the kingdom" (4:23; 9:35) is nothing less than his Father's message to the whole world that there is a way to live out the values of heaven on earth. Jesus embodies the message in word and deed and thereby becomes a model for all who would "follow" him.

Despite the connectedness between the two summary passages, each one also contains a distinct purpose. The present passage (4:23-25) accomplishes two goals immediately prior to the great tract of teaching in the Sermon on the Mount. One goal is to establish that Jesus' threefold ministry of preaching, teaching, and healing are entirely effective. The crowds track him wherever he goes, and they bring him all of their needy because he can cure them. The second goal is to affirm that this efficacy not only secures his reputation in Galilee but also far and wide, beyond the borders of a backwater fishing area, even to Syria, which may have been the home of the Matthean community. The wide appeal of Jesus' message, alluded to at the beginning of his mission, begins to take effect without a hint of the resistance foreshadowed in the story of his birth (2:3,16). The crowds described in such summary passages seem, at first glance, to be favorable to Jesus. But is it merely the odd attraction of novelty or the constant desire to get something for nothing? In the end, the crowds will prove fickle (27:15-23,25). Their portrait throughout the Gospel is ambivalent, running hot and cold. Discipleship is not simply being fascinated by wonders and miracles that defy natural explanations.

The Sermon on the Mount (5:1–7:28)

Chapters five through seven comprise the greatest discourse of Jesus in Matthew and arguably the most impressive sermon in all of Christian history. Its location as the first in the series of five great discourses throughout the Gospel reinforces its status as the pre-eminent sermon. All of the Gospels show Jesus to be a teacher. Mark, for instance, emphasizes Jesus as a teacher by designating him such on a variety of occasions, but interestingly tied more to miracle stories than to great tracts of discourse material (Mk 1:22-27). John, on the other hand, contains long discourses of Jesus, but they often begin in dialogues that switch to soliloquies as Jesus speaks at length about himself and his relation to his heavenly Father (Jn 3:1-21; 6:22-40). Luke also contains a great sermon, the Sermon on the level ground or plain (Lk 6:17-49), most of which parallels Matthew's Sermon in great detail, an indication that the source for the Sermon might be the hypothetical Q document. Yet Luke's Sermon lacks the dramatic setting, the scope, and the artistic balance of Matthew's Sermon. In Matthew's Sermon we encounter Jesus the master teacher, instructing his disciples about a variety of ethical demands that accompany a willingness to follow Jesus.

The setting itself is almost theatrical (5:1-2). Jesus ascends a mountain, the crowds gather round him, he assumes the standard sitting position of a Jewish teacher, and he begins to teach his disciples who come to him. There is a lovely spot in the Holy Land that commemorates this event, the Mount of the Beatitudes near the Sea of Galilee. In this bucolic setting one can envision Jesus teaching on the side of a hill overlooking a tranquil sea. The picture seems to require that the disciples are in the first rows, a group of insiders, surrounded by crowds that overhear what Jesus says. The Sermon's content, however, is transparently directed to disciples of all time. The scene may be likened to a movie in which the action stops and the camera zooms in for a closeup as the main character begins a lengthy discourse containing broad moral ramifications. The story for the moment is suspended. All eyes and ears are focused on Jesus' words.

Structuring the Sermon on the Mount (5:1–7:28) is daunting. Scholars have made a variety of proposals. A possible seven-section outline follows, accompanied by a synopsis of the Sermon's content. Your NAB translation gives helpful headings for each section.

5:1-2   Setting
      Part 1: Signs of the Kingdom of Heaven (5:3-16)
              5:3-12   The Beatitudes
              5:13-16   Discipleship as Salt and Light
      Part 2: The True Nature of the Law and its Fulfillment
              (5:17-48)
              5:17-20   The Fulfillment of the Law
              5:21-26   Anger and Judgment
              5:27-30   Adultery
              5:31-32   Divorce
              5:33-37   Oaths
              5:38-42   Revenge
              5:43-48   Love of enemies
      Part 3: Christian piety and Prayer (6:1-18)
              6:1-4   Almsgiving
              6:5-14   Prayer and the Lord's Prayer
              6:16-18   Fasting
      Part 4: Exhortations for Discipleship (6:19–7:23)
              6:19-21   Treasure in Heaven
              6:22-23   Lamp of the Body
              6:24   God and Mammon
              6:25-34   Dependence on God
               7:1-5   Judging Others
               7:6   Pearls before Swine
               7:7-11   Answer to Prayers

7:12   The Golden Rule
7:13-14   The Narrow Gate
7:15-20   False Prophets and Bad Fruit
7:21-23   True Discipleship

Part 5: The Essential Choice (7:24-27)
        7:24-27   Parable of Firm and Unfirm
                      Foundations

7:28   Reaction

Before explaining the various components of the Sermon I want to make a few general observations to set the context for our interpretation.

First Observation: The Sermon is artificially constructed by the evangelist to represent an ideal instruction. He has gathered various strands of traditions about Jesus' teaching and put them together into an artistic, thematically-unified whole. For example, the setting (5:1-2) and the reaction (7:28) frame the Sermon and place it in the context of the story Matthew tells. Also, the Beatitudes (5:3-12), themselves artistically structured in parallel fashion, begin the Sermon and orient it as an eschatological instruction of God's Law. God is the source of all blessing and teaching about righteousness by means of the Law. What Jesus gives is no less than an understanding of God's will. The final parable on the contrasting houses is meant to summarize the choice that we are given. We may build on rock (God's teaching) or on sand (human weakness). The entire Sermon contrasts these two opposites and reinforces the need for disciples to choose wisely in all that they live.

Second Observation: The Sermon is not a creation out of whole cloth of Jesus' unique teaching. Even less is it a "new Law" in contrast to the "old Law," the Jewish Torah given to Moses on Mount Sinai. The Sermon is tinged throughout with OT background in much of its language and even in its basic conceptions, and the Mosaic imagery evokes the divine origins of

49

Jesus' instruction. Crucial to this question is the understanding of the teaching about the Law (5:17-20). Jesus explicitly says: "Do not think that I have come to abolish the law or the prophets. I have come not to abolish but to fulfill" (5:17). This perspective provides a strong measure of continuity with the OT. The contrast, then, is not between a new and old Law, but the proper interpretation and living out of the Torah, the one Law familiar to Matthew's community. We Christians need to be reminded periodically that the OT is God's Word, too. Not everything in it has been abrogated or surpassed by the NT teaching, even though the ultimate meaning of Jesus' death and resurrection goes far beyond anything the OT envisioned and the NT brings the OT to its fulfillment. When Jesus instructs on many topics that are also found in the Torah, the purpose is to focus our attention on the proper way to live out the spirit and intention of that Law. Jesus himself shows the way and is the key to the potential success of his followers in doing the same.

Third Observation: While the Sermon may not do away with the Jewish Law, it does not merely repeat or rehash it. There is something *new* in the Sermon that provides a measure of discontinuity with the OT. Jesus' teaching radicalizes the Law in many aspects, especially in the sections that begin with the dual phrase: "You have heard that it was said . . . but I say to you . . ." (5:21-22, 27-28, 31-32, 33-34, 38-39, 43-44). Even traditional teachings such as the OT law of revenge (the *lex talionis,* "eye for eye, tooth for tooth"; Ex 21:24; Lev 24:19-20; Dt 19:21) are radicalized. Even if he uses OT themes in his teaching, Jesus nonetheless calls his disciples to a more radical way of living that, in the end, transcends the Law. In typical Jewish style, Matthew's Jesus calls for righteousness (*dikaiosyne*), a traditional OT concept of living an upright ethical life before God and humanity. Yet he calls his disciples to transcend the righteousness lived out in the religion of his day: "I tell you, unless your righteousness surpasses that of the scribes and Pharisees, you will not enter the kingdom of heaven" (5:20). Christians are thus

50

called to a greater righteousness, a theme that permeates Matthew's Gospel. (Matthew uses the adjective "righteous" some seventeen times and the noun "righteousness" seven times.)

Fourth Observation: The Sermon contains a tremendous amount of ethical teaching which makes it tempting to interpret everything from a moralistic standpoint. This impression is unavoidable, and most of the Sermon contains moral instruction that is fairly easy to grasp though difficult to live. This moral perspective, however, is not the sole way to read the Sermon on the Mount. It also has a *christological* perspective that should not be overlooked. As Matthew presents it, when Jesus delivers the Sermon he is essentially fulfilling his identity as God's Son. His words reveal that he both knows and understands God's Word, unlike the religious leaders of Israel who have shown themselves to be negligent and even warped in their duties. Thus, the Sermon says as much about Jesus and his ability to expound on his Father's will as it does about us who hear the instruction and are challenged to put it into practice as the greater righteousness.

With these general comments in mind, we now examine sections of the Sermon on the Mount for their individual teachings.

The Beatitudes of the Sermon on the Mount (5:1-16)

> [1] When he saw the crowds, he went up the mountain, and after he had sat down, his disciples came to him.
> [2] He began to teach them, saying:
> [3] "Blessed are the poor in spirit,
> for theirs is the kingdom of heaven.
> [4] Blessed are they who mourn,
> for they will be comforted.
> [5] Blessed are the meek,
> for they will inherit the land.

⁶ Blessed are they who hunger and thirst for
    righteousness,
for they will be satisfied.
⁷ Blessed are the merciful,
for they will be shown mercy.
⁸ Blessed are the clean of heart,
for they will see God.
⁹ Blessed are the peacemakers,
for they will be called children of God.
¹⁰ Blessed are they who are persecuted for the sake of
    righteousness,
for theirs is the kingdom of heaven.
   ¹¹ Blessed are you when they insult you and persecute you
and utter every kind of evil against you [falsely] because of
me. ¹² Rejoice and be glad, for your reward will be great in
heaven. Thus they persecuted the prophets who were before
you."

The first major part of the Sermon consists of the Beatitudes
and images of discipleship (5:3-16). Almost every Christian is
taught to memorize the *eight* Beatitudes from Matthew's
Gospel. Look again. How many times does the word "blessed"
(or, in some translations the weaker expression, "happy")
occur? If we count only eight, then we are referring only to those
in the third person plural (5:3-10). But verses 11-12 record
another Beatitude containing the second person plural,
"Blessed are you . . ." At this point the Beatitudes clearly
become directed to the primary hearers of the Sermon, the
disciples themselves. They are warned that their opting for
discipleship will bring them suffering and persecution, something in line with Jesus' own destiny and with the prophets
before him. Even here, in a section devoted primarily to the
comfort of those who find themselves shortchanged in this
world, a warning of the sacrifices which must be made to follow
Jesus rears its head.
   The eight Beatitudes are themselves carefully structured.
Each begins with the same word "blessed." This word is

common in the wisdom literature of the OT. It constitutes both a statement and a wish that God's blessing be upon someone in this life. In this instance, the blessing is pronounced for existing conditions but the reward is promised in the life hereafter. These Beatitudes are eschatological in orientation. The first and last Beatitudes repeat the reward of the kingdom, while the fourth and eighth Beatitudes mention righteousness. These two concepts of God's kingdom and righteousness not only frame the Beatitudes but are essentially key concepts in the whole Sermon on the Mount. From one perspective, the Sermon represents God's will expressed in Jesus' words, a vision of the "kingdom." From another perspective these words challenge people to live by a more radical ethical standard of righteousness. Two primary religious directions, vertical (God) and horizontal (humanity), are thereby preserved. In addition, the first set of four is directed inwardly toward attitudes (poor in spirit, mourn, meek, hunger and thirst for righteousness), while the second set of four is directed outwardly toward actions either given or received (merciful, clean of heart, peacemakers, persecuted for righteousness). Thus, two directions within humanity are preserved, the interior that controls attitudes, and the exterior that controls behavior.

In comparison to Luke's smaller list of four Beatitudes (6:20-22), Matthew has spiritualized the contents somewhat (cf. poor in spirit vs. "poor"; hungry for righteousness vs. "now hungry"). Perhaps Matthew's community had fewer people than Luke's who were physically poor, hungry, and homeless. Luke's Gospel has many more passages dealing with the concrete needs in life than does Matthew; it also has a penchant for emphasizing the "here and now." Yet I do not think Matthew has taken the edge off of the Beatitudes to make them some sort of ethical "pie in the sky" that does not relate to daily life. Rather, Matthew's primary concern is to change attitudes internally that can then affect a change in behavior outwardly. Matthew's concept of righteousness is very concrete. It implies putting into practice the expressed intentions of the Law. This cannot be achieved unless people have their priorities properly in order: "But seek first the kingdom [of God] and his righteousness, and all these things will be given you besides" (6:33).

Some of the concepts themselves derive from OT passages that form the backdrop of Jesus' teaching:

- poor in spirit and mourners (Is 61:1-3)
- the meek (Ps 37:11)
- clean of heart (Ps 24:4)
- hunger and thirst for righteousness (Ps 107:5,9).

The most urgent question of interpreting the Beatitudes is how to understand them generically. There may be as many interpretations of them as there are interpreters. A quick list summarizes the most popular options:

1) the most complete and elegant summary of Christian ethics
2) impossible ideals for humanity that can never be achieved
3) ideal values intended only for disciples of Jesus
4) goals to work toward in life and that are possible to achieve but with difficulty
5) wishful blessings upon those who suffer or are in need
6) the values of God's kingdom when it finally arrives.

Whatever preference one chooses, the essential question to begin with is how you see these blessings functioning within the story Matthew tells. Once that context is honored, I believe further interpretation falls into place. The Beatitudes encompass many values that go beyond Christian parameters. Yet it is Jesus himself, in Matthew's story, who embodies these values and invites his followers to do the same. Many saints through the ages have attempted to live by these values, notably Francis of Assisi, Martin de Porres, and Therese of Lisieux. Perhaps in our own day we might point to Mother Theresa of Calcutta. Their histories are often filled with suffering, pain, persecution, ridicule, and even martyrdom. However one finally understands the Beatitudes, they have become a benchmark of Christian living and they still provide a convenient checklist of attitudes and behaviors that help us measure our progress toward the kingdom of God. To be a disciple of Jesus is to be properly oriented toward God's perspective. It truly requires being different in a world that promotes conformity. For wealthy, Western cultures, the Sermon on the Mount makes a strong counter cultural statement.

[13] "You are the salt of the earth. But if salt loses its taste, with what can it be seasoned? It is no longer good for anything but to be thrown out and trampled underfoot.

[14] "You are the light of the world. A city set on a mountain cannot be hidden. [15] Nor do they light a lamp and then put it under a bushel basket; it is set on a lampstand, where it gives light to all in the house. [16] Just so, your light must shine before others, that they may see your good deeds and glorify your heavenly Father."

On the heels of the Beatitudes comes a metaphor that compares the disciples to three images from daily life: salt, city and light. Jesus does not simply draw the comparison, as if the disciples are *like* salt and light. They *are* salt and light. And as a city cannot be hidden, neither can disciples remain behind the scenes. They have to stand out, stand up and be counted. Their message is intended for the world to see. Like salt, they need to spark "flavor" in life, that is, be an instrument for the best to come to the fore. Like salt that was also used to light cooking fires, they are called to be catalysts to light the fire of faith. Their lives are to shed light in the world, to be beacons of hope and models of inspiration. These are simple but attractive images. They never let us forget that discipleship places demands upon us that can influence the world. If we fail to live up to the vision, we are as useless as flat, lifeless salt. If the

Beatitudes laid out a vision of an attitudinal and behavioral shift required of disciples, these metaphors on discipleship concretize the mission outwardly. They must be a visible example for others.

The next large section of the Sermon (5:17-48) contains two subdivisions. The first part (5:17-20) sets forth the basic approach to the Law that I described above. Jesus has not come to do away with it but to fulfill it. Yet his ability to do so has ramifications for the disciples, for they are immediately called to a greater righteousness that will surpass anything Israel ever encountered. This general statement is followed by a lengthy second part that indicates the content of what greater righteousness will entail (5:21-48). These are commonly called the six antitheses because of the form they take: "You have heard it said . . . but I say to you . . ." The topics covered include:

- killing and anger

- adultery and lust

- divorce and adultery

- false oaths and not taking oaths

- retaliation and surrender to violence

- love and hate.

On Adultery and Divorce (5:27-32)

[27] "You have heard that it was said, 'You shall not commit adultery.' [28] But I say to you, everyone who looks at a woman with lust has already committed adultery with her in his heart. [29] If your right eye causes you to sin, tear it out and throw it away. It is better for you to lose one of your members than to have your whole body thrown into Gehenna.

According to each topic, regardless of what the OT Law taught, Jesus teaches that he expects a stricter alternative to be normative for those who join him. In this regard Jesus is not a minimalist. There are no shortcuts to true righteousness. The span of topics extends in various directions. The Law prohibited killing, but Jesus says that even remaining angry with someone will bring about judgment (5:21-26). The Law prohibited adultery, but Jesus notes that even lusting after a woman in your heart is paramount to adultery (5:27-30). We cannot overlook the male perspective here, typical of most of the biblical literature, especially from within the Jewish tradition. Although the text reads as if it is only directed to men who lust for women, from a Christian perspective the regulation applies equally to men and women. This Christian insight developed slowly over time after the NT period. Here we see the focus is again attitudinal. Attitudes can affect behavior, so Jesus expects the highest possible standard to prevail.

> [30] "And if your right hand causes you to sin, cut it off and throw it away. It is better for you to lose one of your members than to have your whole body go into Gehenna. [31] It was also said, 'Whoever divorces his wife must give her a bill of divorce.' [32] But I say to you, whoever divorces his wife (unless the marriage is unlawful) causes her to commit adultery, and whoever marries a divorced woman commits adultery."

The practice of divorce is the next topic to be altered (5:31-32). Jewish Law permitted divorce. That is to say, men could divorce their wives. This was an intense issue in Jesus' day, and there were at least two differing views among the Jews about divorce. One was strict on the reasons one needed for divorce, the other was lenient. Jesus, however, goes beyond them both and prohibits any divorce, with one exception, *porneia*. The NAB translates this word "unless the marriage is unlawful" (5:32), but it may mean more literally "sexual irregularity or misconduct" on the woman's part. The exact meaning of the term is hotly contested. Actually, Matthew treats the entire question of divorce more extensively elsewhere in the context of a theology of marriage (19:1-12). There the perspective remains basically the same. Jesus taught that lawful marriage was indissoluble because God had made it so. Apparently, either Matthew or his community felt it necessary to adapt Jesus' teaching for pastoral purposes. The exception clause creates a loophole in the absolutely-no-divorce rule. If there are criteria by which a marriage can be seen as unlawful, then divorce may be permitted in some instances. Given the tremendous pastoral problem of divorce and remarriage in our own day, we should examine this issue a bit further.

Scholars agree that the historical Jesus forbade divorce. This was exceptional within Judaism which permitted divorce under certain circumstances. Very early in the Christian tradition, exceptions to Jesus' absolute rule appeared. The earliest exception is found in Paul's letters. When writing to his beloved Corinthians who were much troubled by various moral matters in their society, Paul wrote that normally divorce was not a good thing (1 Cor 7:12-14). However, he indicates that an exception might be made when an unbeliever chooses to depart for the sake of peace in the family (1 Cor 7:15). Paul emphasizes that his entire discussion of marriage and divorce in this section of the letter is his own view and not something from "the Lord" (1 Cor 7:12). Paul's pastoral sensitivity has not been lost on the Catholic Church which uses the Corinthian passage to justify its practice of "the Pauline privilege" which permits just such a circumstance. The Church has also evolved its practice over the centuries, in the form of marriage annulments, to recognize that the very origin of some marriages is faulty and invalid, even though problems may not manifest themselves until much later in the marriage. Canon law regulates the response to such circumstances, and the result is not a divorce but a declaration of nullity of the marriage. This leaves the partners free to engage in another marriage, hopefully one more suitable, long-lasting and well prepared.

How does Matthew fit into this scene? My digression was to set out the context in which I think we can see Matthew's contribution to this delicate question. Clearly, since at least biblical times, marriage has been problematic. On the one hand, the ideal stated in Genesis about the goal of marriage (Gn 2:24), reiterated more firmly in Jesus' own teaching (Mt 19:4-6), is a sacred trust that should not be broken. On the other hand, Matthew's Gospel is another witness to the practical need to make adaptations to this ideal in certain restricted instances. In a society such as ours, which has difficulty making any kind of firm commitment and which permits or even encourages serial marriages and divorces, Matthew cannot be used as a warrant for licentiousness. Rather, Matthew's community (perhaps relying on earlier Christian tradition) responded to a pastoral situation that warranted, in their judgment, a modification of Jesus' teaching. The fact that it now stands in the Bible as part of God's Word indicates that it found general acceptance in time in the universal Church. In the midst of a Sermon that calls us to the ideal, this little passage is a reminder that our best attempts to live out the ideal sometimes fall short. At times, pastoral sensitivity takes precedence over rigid conformity. Since Matthew's own Jesus rails against legalism and placing excessive burdens on people (23:4,23-24), I suspect he would be very comfortable with the way Matthew adapted the teaching to his own day.

Oaths, Retaliation, and Love of Enemies (5:33-48)

The next parts of these antitheses address successively the issues of oaths (5:33-37), retaliation (5:38-42), and love of enemies (5:43-48). Disciples of Jesus have no need for oaths, for they should say what they mean and mean what they say. Utter honesty is the norm. When it comes to vengeance, which was permitted within degrees in the OT, Jesus radicalizes the message considerably. Turning the other cheek, going the extra mile, handing over your coat as well as your shirt (the reverse order of what we would expect, as seen in Luke 6:29—". . . from the person who takes your cloak, do not withhold even your tunic"), all are Christian actions that go beyond what seems reasonable. The radicalization of the *lex talionis,* the law of commensurate retaliation (vv. 38-39), is particularly striking. Many Christians today quote this OT law to justify capital punishment without making any reference whatsoever to Jesus' severe modification of it. This teaching, coupled with the climactic one on love of enemies (5:43-48), provides the pacifistic core of Jesus' teaching. The larger goal is clear: "So be perfect, just as your heavenly Father is perfect" (5:48). These words can be very troubling to anyone who struggles with perfectionism. But this is not a license to be perfectionistic as described by psychologists. The Greek word perfect (*teleios*) implies more the goal toward which one is moving. A better sense might be, "be perfected as your heavenly Father is perfect." It is process-oriented. It means that we can never stop trying to live out better the vision that Jesus has set forth in the Sermon.

The Our Father (6:1-13)

[1] "[But] take care not to perform righteous deeds in order that people may see them; otherwise, you will have no recompense from your heavenly Father. [2] When you give alms, do not blow a trumpet before you, as the hypocrites do in the synagogues and in the streets to win the praise of others. Amen, I say to you, they have received their reward. [3] But when you give alms, do not let your left hand know what your right is doing, [4] so that your almsgiving may be secret. And your Father who sees in secret will repay you.

[5] "When you pray, do not be like the hypocrites, who love to stand and pray in the synagogues and on street corners so that others may see them. Amen, I say to you, they have received their reward. [6] But when you pray, go to your inner room, close the door, and pray to your Father in secret. And

your Father who sees in secret will repay you. [7] In praying, do not babble like the pagans, who think that they will be heard because of their many words. [8] Do not be like them. Your Father knows what you need before you ask him. [9] 'This is how you are to pray:

> Our Father in heaven,
> hallowed be your name,
> [10] your kingdom come,
> your will be done,
> on earth as in heaven.
> [11] Give us today our daily bread;
> [12] and forgive us our debts,
> as we forgive our debtors;
> [13] and do not subject us to the final test,
> but deliver us from the evil one.' "

With chapter six the Sermon takes a slightly different turn to focus on some deeds with specifically religious overtones. This third major section deals with Christian prayer and piety (6:1-18). These include almsgiving (6:1-4), prayer (6:5-15), and fasting (6:16-18). In each instance a contrast is made with "hypocrites" who do exactly what Jesus' followers are to avoid (the expression again, "I say to you . . ."). In regard to almsgiving, the normal practice was to draw attention to the pious donation to the needy, whether in public places or in the synagogue. Jesus' disciples, however, should give secretly, for God knows in secret what each of us does and will reward the almsgiver. Jesus likewise expresses a similar approach to fasting (vv. 16-18). In regard to prayer, hypocrites love to display their prayerfulness in public. In contrast, disciples should go to their room, shut the door and pray in private. God hears all. Also, they should not rattle on like pagans trying to get a hearing. Rather, they should pray succinctly and simply. Then Jesus gives the prayer that, despite its thoroughly Jewish character, has become the hallmark of Christian prayer, the Lord's Prayer or Our Father (6:9-13). It might better be termed "the disciples' prayer," for it is given to the disciples as their model prayer.

Even though God knows what we need before we ask (6:8), that should not stop us from praying. Prayer is primarily for us, not God. Our prayers of praise add nothing to God's greatness, yet they express what we should proclaim as creatures of God. Our prayers of request, on the other hand, demonstrate our utter confidence in God.

The Our Father is a prayer that models the very best in what constitutes quality prayer. It is short and succinct (woe to us long-winded preachers!); it focuses on God (vv. 9-10) and on our fellow human beings (v. 12); it expresses concrete needs such as "daily bread" (v. 11); and it pleads for exemption from the time of testing (v. 13). It also shows that Jesus desires earnestly to share his personal relationship with God as Father with us. We are taught to pray "*Our* Father in heaven" (cf. "your [heavenly] Father," 5:16,48; 6:4,6,8,15,18 etc.). While Jesus retains his unique identity as God's Son, as disciples we are nevertheless given a share in that special relationship. The Our Father is such a profound prayer that it should be reflected on at length. We are so accustomed to it that we can easily overlook its riches. Each phrase contains deeper mysteries than the simple words that communicate them. I recommend a slow, careful reflection on each part of this prayer that has become like a Christian ID badge.

True Riches, Avoiding Judgment, and the Golden Rule (6:19-23)

After these important instructions on Christian piety, the Sermon shifts to a series of random topics that round out Jesus' eschatological teaching. This fourth section focuses on exhortations for discipleship (6:19–7:23). There is no obvious structure to the rest of the Sermon, yet it fleshes out aspects of Christian living that are essential to authentic discipleship. These include not storing up earthly treasures but heavenly ones (6:19-21), the power of light over darkness (6:22-23), not splitting our allegiance between God and mammon (the

Aramaic word for money, 6:24), not worrying excessively about physical needs such as food and clothing (6:25-34), not judging others when we should acknowledge our own faults first (7:1-5), not wasting our spiritual resources on those who have no respect for holiness (the mysterious saying about dogs and pigs, 7:6), trusting that God will indeed answer our prayers if we would request them (7:7-11; note the verbs ask, seek, knock), and the "Golden Rule" to do unto others what we would want done to us (7:12).

In the midst of these admonitions Jesus uses a term that is a Matthean favorite to describe the disciples: "you of little faith" (*oligopistoi*, 6:30; cf. 8:26; 14:31; 16:8). The expression provides a clue how we are to understand this series of instructions. One might view each of these instructions as practical, spiritual advice that would emerge naturally from any great teacher of wisdom. Yet they are part of a larger picture in which Jesus is establishing the parameters of discipleship. We may be tempted sometimes to settle for "little faith" or minimalism. Discipleship demands great faith, personal trust in Jesus and his teaching. This becomes even clearer in the last section of the Sermon where Jesus gives a series of warnings about the nature of true discipleship (7:13-27).

The final instructions in the Sermon turn to explicit warnings that indicate discipleship is neither easy nor comfortable. The gate through which one enters is narrow and those who can accomplish it are few (7:13-14). If you have worried about the "numbers" game, how few people respond to invitations for religious events or the crisis in religious vocations or the lack of Church influence in resolving critical moral issues in society, these words are a good reminder that Jesus warned that success would not come easy. Not only that, but there are false prophets around, wolves in sheep's clothing, who would lead us off track (7:15-20). Employing an OT metaphor that is tied to his understanding of Christian conversion, Matthew invokes the image of a tree bearing fruit. Good trees (=good people) bear only good fruit (=good actions). Actions speak louder than words. If one's actions are bad (=bad fruit), despite their words, such a person is not an authentic disciple (=bad tree). This is another example of Matthew attempting to bring internal attitudes and external attitudes into harmony. You cannot say you believe one way when your actions betray your true motivations. Finally, in a passage that presages the great judgment scene in his last great sermon (25:31-46), Jesus says that discipleship is not a mere matter of crying out "Lord, Lord" in order to enter God's kingdom (7:21-23). Rather, doing the Father's will is what is essential (v. 21; cf. 12:50; 21:31). This is a forceful way for Jesus to insist that one's moral behavior in conformity to God's will is what will determine one's ultimate fate in the kingdom to come.

The Two Foundations (7:24-29)

[24] "Everyone who listens to these words of mine and acts on them will be like a wise man who built his house on rock. [25] The rain fell, the floods came, and the winds blew and buffeted the house. But it did not collapse; it had been set solidly on rock. [26] And everyone who listens to these words of mine but does not act on them will be like a fool who built his house on sand. [27] The rain fell, the floods came, and the winds blew and buffeted the house. And it collapsed and was completely ruined."

[28] When Jesus finished these words, the crowds were astonished at his teaching, [29] for he taught them as one having authority, and not as their scribes.

These four warnings lead to the climax of the entire Sermon, the parable of the two houses (7:24-27). Listening to Jesus' words and putting them into practice is compared to building a house on rock. The secure foundation will ensure that it withstands even the most ferocious storm. The opposite is also true. Only a fool builds a house on a sandy beach without a firm foundation. If one chooses to ignore Jesus' words or fails to put them into action, just about any storm will blow it away. Note that

Jesus does not include a direct admonition to build your house on a firm foundation. The message is implicit in the telling of the story. Coming, as it does, at the conclusion of the Sermon on the Mount, we can see that Jesus leaves us with an option. Discipleship entails responding to Jesus' call. It requires both hearing and doing what God wills (v. 24). Yet we have a choice to make. From Matthew's perspective the choice is only twofold. Either you follow God and God's ways, or you revert to human foibles. The one path leads to eternal reward, the other to destruction. In an old Peanuts cartoon by Charles Shulz, I remember Linus telling Lucy "You are going to reap just what you sow." Snoopy, who overhears the conversation, is shown walking away with his head down and saying to himself, "I'd like to see a little more margin for error." We might like to see a bit more room for the "gray areas" of life. That is not an option in the Matthean world view.

There is an "escape valve" built into the Sermon that Matthew discusses later (the teaching on reconciliation and forgiveness, cf. 6:12,14-15; 18:21-22), but the general perspective of the Sermon is that the choice itself is very narrow. In a sense, it offers dual visions. One vision, limited by human potential, leads to self-destruction. The other, because it originates with God, leads to salvation. Matthew's Jesus elsewhere expresses this overarching principle: "For human beings this is impossible, but for God all things are possible" (19:26; cf. 16:23). This dualistic approach is characteristic of some OT literature, such as the wisdom and apocalyptic literature, and the Dead Sea scrolls, so we should not be surprised to find it in Matthew. Its purpose is not to frighten us but to set forth clearly the ultimate options. Jesus promotes mature accountability in his teachings. The crowd's response to Jesus is one of astonishment because his words had authority unlike their own religious leaders (7:28-29). But amazement at Jesus is not what constitutes discipleship. One must make a conscious decision to follow Jesus. We are either for or against him. We either follow God's ways or we go our own. The Sermon on the Mount enunciates the challenge in bold relief. We now know what we are getting into, but the implications have yet to be played out in Matthew's story. Jesus has shown himself to be God's Son in Word, now he moves on to show that his understanding of God's will is not an illusion. He will demonstrate his stance in action.

III

The Healing and Teaching
Ministry of Jesus
(8:1–11:1)

With Jesus' lengthy discourse at an end, the plot of the story resumes. The camera, as it were, swings into action again. The text moves from Jesus' authority in word to a series of miracle stories that demonstrate Jesus' power and authority in deed (8:1–9:38). Jesus' demand that his disciples both hear and do what he teaches (7:24) is nothing less than he himself accomplishes. The miracles are collected into three groups of three stories each, interrupted by short sections that provide summary passages or that focus on examples of discipleship, positively and negatively. Some miracles show Jesus' power to heal, others demonstrate his power over demons, still others show his power over nature. How are we to approach miracle stories in our day? Before proceeding to specific details, I will again offer a few general observations to guide our spiritual reflection.

First, there are two temptations in treating the miracle stories of the Gospels. One is to assume that they are to be understood literally in every detail just as they are recorded. Hence, some fundamentalist interpreters will do exegetical contortions to justify this or that detail of a miracle story, allegedly in order to protect the integrity of the Word of God. The other temptation is, as scientifically educated people, to dismiss the stories out of hand. In this approach, some see miracles as a remnant of a pre-scientific age that did not know any better. Neither approach helps us in a spiritual interpretation of the Gospel. We should avoid both temptations. There is an intermediate approach. We should not pre-judge the material but pay attention to its function within the story Matthew tells. Our modern preoccupation to probe "what really happened" has to be resisted. Instead, we have to examine the religious message contained in such stories.

Second, all the Synoptic Gospels share a common background with regard to miracle stories. The evangelists lived in a time and culture that assumed the reality of miracles. There are many examples of heroes in ancient literature, both Jewish and Greco-Roman, who could perform miraculous deeds. The Gospels fit into this context. Some stories even have explicit OT background in similar stories (e.g., the stories of Elisha in 2 Kgs 4:18-37,42-44). Assumptions include that many human illnesses were caused by demons and attributed to some evildoing on the part of the recipient, that some human beings possessed special powers to overcome such situations, and that God often directly intervened in human affairs to set things right or to punish wrongdoing. This cultural context helped to shape the Gospel material, but when comparisons are made to other ancient miracle stories, the Gospels still contain unique aspects unexplained by mere literary conventions. The Gospel miracles exhibit an intense interest in christological assertions not found in secular miracle stories of other Jewish or Hellenistic miracle workers.

Third, many Gospel healing stories contain a similar pattern. This indicates the genre of the story. The most common elements are:

- request for a healing on the part of the ill person or a representative, including a description of the illness
- dialogue with Jesus or verbal response
- contact with Jesus effects the miracle itself
- astonished reaction of bystanders and the spreading of Jesus' reputation.

Sometimes the miracle is attributed by Jesus to the faith of the recipient (8:13; 9:22,29), but Matthew also makes it clear that Jesus possessed extraordinary power to accomplish miracles. The pattern helps us see the main purpose of all the miracle stories—to demonstrate that Jesus is the authoritative Son of God (and Son of David, a title particularly tied to healings) who has power over demons and all evil because God has granted it to him (cf. 11:27). The primary purpose, then, is christological rather than moral. The miracles confirm Jesus' identity and provide the appropriate credentials for the messiah.

Fourth, a common misunderstanding of Gospel miracle stories is to think that they were primarily to prove in concrete fashion that Jesus was God, and thus bring people to faith. This is, in fact, the clear perspective of John's Gospel regarding the "signs" that Jesus performed (not "miracles"; see Jn 6:14,30; 12:18). In John Jesus' miraculous signs are meant to bring people to faith. But this is not the perspective of Matthew. Miracles are themselves ambiguous and prove nothing. Yes, some people are brought to faith through them, but more often the reaction is one of amazement and awe, which are not the same as true faith. People have often asked me why, if Jesus performed so many miracles, more people did not believe in him. They assume that if they witnessed such miracles, they would also come to faith. But the fact is that Christianity began with a very small group of people who had faith. Even today, when it comes to miracles of unexplainable cures of cancer or other illnesses, some people will refuse to acknowledge the miraculous and assume the cause is human but merely not understood. Others perhaps are always seeking the miraculous as the main evidence that God is active in human affairs. This can lead to holding God hostage: "Show me that you love me, Lord; answer my prayers *my* way." Neither approach works. The key to unlocking the meaning of miracles remains, as it always has, with one's faith in God's power to extend beyond the limits of the natural world. Let's look at how Matthew puts the miracle stories to work in his Gospel.

An outline of this section of the Gospel shows the balanced structure.

Part 1: The First Set of Three miracles (8:1-15)
      8:2-4   Cleansing a Leper
      8:5-13   Healing a Centurion's Servant
      8:14-15   Healing Peter's Mother-in-Law
      8:16-22   First Digression: Would-Be Followers
Part 2: The Second Set of Three Miracles (8:23–9:8)
      8:23-27   Calming of a Storm at Sea
      8:28-34   Healing Two Men Possessed by Demons
      9:1-8   Healing a Paralyzed Person
      9:9-17   Second Digression: Call of Matthew
Part 3: The Third Set of Three Miracles (9:18-34)
      9:18-26   Healing an Official's Daughter and the Woman with a Hemorrhage
      9:27-31   Healing Two Blind Men
      9:32-34   Healing a Mute Person
      9:35-38   Final Digression: Summary of Jesus' Compassion

Cleansing a Leper (8:1-4)

[1] When Jesus came down from the mountain, great crowds followed him. [2] And then a leper approached, did him homage, and said, "Lord, if you wish, you can make me clean." [3] He stretched out his hand, touched him, and said, "I will do it. Be made clean." His leprosy was cleansed immediately. [4] Then Jesus said to him, "See that you tell no one, but go show yourself to the priest, and offer the gift that Moses prescribed; that will be proof for them."

The first miracle story, the healing of a leper, is told in Spartan simplicity (8:1-4). Jesus descends the mountain in Galilee where he has taught, accompanied by crowds. A leper approaches him indicating by his demeanor that he is predisposed to Jesus' healing power, for he "did him homage, and said 'Lord, if you wish, you can make me clean'" (8:2). The Greek verb "worship" or "do homage" (*proskyneo*) is a favorite Matthean word for the proper disposition toward Jesus (cf. 2:2,8,11; 14:33; 28:17). The leper, a pariah in the Greco-Roman world, is ripe for healing, for he is not only in need but trusts that Jesus can cure him. Faith and the boldness to act on it are both part of the miracle setting. He puts his trust in Jesus but also leaves room for Jesus' own desire to assist someone in need.

Healing a Centurion's Servant (8:5-13)

[5] When he entered Capernaum, a centurion approached him and appealed to him, [6] saying, "Lord, my servant is lying at home paralyzed, suffering dreadfully." [7] He said to him, "I will come and cure him." [8] The centurion said in reply, "Lord, I am not worthy to have you enter under my roof; only say the word and my servant will be healed. [9] For I too am a person subject to authority, with soldiers subject to me. And I say to one, 'Go,' and he goes; and to another, 'Come here,' and he comes; and to my slave, 'Do this,' and he does it." [10] When Jesus heard this, he was amazed and said to those following him, "Amen, I say to you, in no one in Israel have I found such faith. [11] I say to you, many will come from the east and the west, and will recline with Abraham, Isaac, and Jacob at the banquet in the kingdom of heaven, [12] but the children of the kingdom will be driven out into the outer darkness, where there will be wailing and grinding of teeth." [13] And Jesus said to the centurion, "You may go; as you have believed, let it be done for you." And at that very hour [his] servant was healed.

The next story takes place in Capernaum, a Galilean town by the sea, where Matthew locates Jesus' home (4:13). For the first time a non-Jew, in fact, a Roman centurion, approaches Jesus with a request to heal his servant who is elsewhere (8:5-13). This story is much more detailed than the previous one. The dialogue between Jesus and the centurion is more developed, but the real importance of the story is found in verses 10-11.

Jesus astonishingly commends the centurion's faith and contrasts it with the comparable lack of faith in Israel. Jesus' words hark back to the beginning of the Gospel when we were told that Jesus was also son of Abraham and thus would fulfill the OT hope that Abraham would be the father of many nations, because the gospel would eventually extend to the Gentile world (1:1; 4:15; 8:11; 28:18-20). Even in the midst of the Galilean ministry, Jesus' reputation begins to broaden. The centurion becomes the first exemplar of the faith that eventually went far beyond the bounds of Israel. This miracle story, then, has a dual message. It affirms Jesus' ability to heal even from a distance. A version of the centurion's words, in fact, have entered eucharistc liturgy and speak of recognition that we are unworthy of Jesus' ministrations: "Lord, I am not worthy to have you enter under my roof; only say the word and my servant will be healed" (8:8). And, secondly, the story says that Jesus' message is not restricted to any one people or any given time. Both the message of humility and the need for openness to God's power to blow where it wills retain their appeal in our own day.

Peter's Mother-in-Law and Other Miracles (8:14-17)

¹⁴ Jesus entered the house of Peter, and saw his mother-in-law lying in bed with a fever. ¹⁵ He touched her hand, the fever left her, and she rose and waited on him.

¹⁶ When it was evening, they brought him many who were possessed by demons, and he drove out the spirits by a word and cured all the sick, ¹⁷ to fulfill what had been said by Isaiah the prophet:

"He took away our infirmities
and bore our diseases."

Jesus' compassion for outsiders is equaled by his concern for those close to him. The third story in the first set describes his healing of Peter's mother-in-law (8:14-15). Bereft of all details, it narrates Jesus' healing touch and the mother-in-law's respectful ministering to Jesus in return. The expression "waited on" (*diakonein* = to serve) is paradoxical, for Jesus is the one who came to serve (20:28). Sometimes that is all we need—to let the Lord reach out and touch whatever needs to be cured. The miracle is followed by the first digression which contains two parts, a fulfillment citation and a passage on discipleship. The former passage shows that Jesus' healing ministry was a sign of fulfilling a prophetic word from Isaiah (8:16-17; Is 53:4). Because this is the first fulfillment citation in the Gospel since the infancy narrative, it reinforces in the midst of Jesus' healing ministry that all is occurring under God's direction. That the quotation is from a passage in Isaiah which describes the anonymous suffering servant also hints of the suffering that Jesus will endure because of his ministry. Jesus' mission is not his own but the fulfillment of his Father's will, and it will finally take him to the passion. His desire to bear our sinfulness and to heal our infirmities will culminate in his greatest act of sacrifice, the gift of his life on the cross for our salvation from sin (1:21; 26:28).

The First Digression (8:18-22)

[8] When Jesus saw a crowd around him, he gave orders to cross to the other side. [19] A scribe approached and said to him, "Teacher, I will follow you wherever you go." [20] Jesus answered him, "Foxes have dens and birds of the sky have nests, but the Son of Man has nowhere to rest his head." [21] Another of [his] disciples said to him, "Lord, let me go first and bury my father." [22] But Jesus answered him, "Follow me, and let the dead bury their dead."

The latter passage centers on discipleship again. Matthew clearly indicates that the miracles took place in the company of crowds (8:1,18). These actions no doubt caused some excitement and enthusiasm. It is not surprising, then, to find some people suddenly volunteering to accompany Jesus (8:18-22). One anonymous would-be follower, a scribe, offers to follow Jesus wherever he goes (v. 19). But he does not realize that discipleship is not for volunteers but for those who hear and respond to Jesus' call. Jesus' response to him may strike us as mysterious at best, or even harsh. That "the Son of Man has nowhere to rest his head" is acknowledgment that ministry entails many sacrifices, including itinerant preaching. Another volunteer scribe wants time to settle his affairs before joining Jesus, including the serious obligation to bury his father. For Jews and Gentiles alike, the duty of family burials was sacred, not something to be tossed aside quickly. That, however, is the problem with volunteers. They want to set their own agenda and accomplish their duties in their own time. Jesus will have none of it. Discipleship is response to a call. Witnessing miracles, gaining enthusiasm, and blithely volunteering are not sufficient. Desire alone does not create a disciple. Jesus says starkly: "Follow me and let the dead bury their dead" (v. 22).

Calming a Storm at Sea (8:23-27)

[23] He got into a boat and his disciples followed him. [24] Suddenly a violent storm came up on the sea, so that the boat was being swamped by waves; but he was asleep. [25] They came and woke him, saying, "Lord, save us! We are perishing!" [26] He said to them, "Why are you terrified, O you of little faith?" Then he got up, rebuked the winds and the sea, and there was great calm. [27] The men were amazed and said, "What sort of man is this, whom even the winds and the sea obey?"

Then begins another set of three of miracle stories in which Jesus demonstrates his awesome power (8:23–9:8). The first set was devoted to healings. This next set begins with a nature miracle and moves to healings. The story of the calming of the storm on the sea (8:23-27) is more symbolic than is apparent.

This is noticeable, in part, by the use of a Greek expression meaning literally "large earthquake" (NAB "violent storm") used to describe the storm that besieges the little fishing boat (v. 24). The word alludes to the stupendous signs that accompany Jesus' birth, ministry and death (2:2; 21:10; 27:51-53). It also evokes the image of the violent sea which held great terror for the ancients and which only God could control (Ps 107:23-30).

Jesus, God-with-us, will demonstrate that he has that same power. The boat in this instance represents the Church. His disciples get in the boat with Jesus and go out on the lake. When a bad storm arises that threatens to swamp the boat, they cry out to the sleeping Jesus, "Lord, save us!" (v. 25), liturgical language that is still used in liturgy. Their need to be saved, whether they know it or not, is not merely from the buffeting of this world but from their failure to have full faith. Jesus calls them again, "you of little faith" (8:24). Note that he does not accuse them of having no faith. Rather, their faith is not sufficient yet to sustain their commitment. The Church finds itself periodically in the same boat, so to speak. Certainly Matthew's nascent Christian community felt enormous pressures. Buffeted here and there by strong secular forces, running at times on limited resources, plagued occasionally by doubts and questions, the little ship of the Church seems about to sink. That is when faith becomes most crucial, believing that Jesus will not let us perish but can reinforce our faith and settle the threatening elements at the same time. Just as God could settle the cosmos (Ps 89:9-10), so can Jesus calm the forces that threaten to sink the struggling community of disciples.

In the wake of Vatican Council II many people felt that the Church was sinking. The solid, unchanging Church they had known suddenly was shifting in ways unexpected. Some have tried to take matters in their own hands to correct what they perceive as infidelity to the Church's obligations. They want to stabilize the rocking boat on their own. That is not the way of responsible discipleship. One must have faith in the Lord who can calm the waters.

Two Miracles and the Second Digression (8:28–9:17)

[28] When he came to the other side, to the territory of the Gadarenes, two demoniacs who were coming from the tombs met him. They were so savage that no one could travel by that road. [29]They cried out, "What have you to do with us, Son of God? Have you come here to torment us before the appointed time?" [30]Some distance away a herd of many swine was feeding. [31]The demons pleaded with him, "If you drive us out, send us into the herd of swine." [32]And he said to them, "Go then!" They came out and entered the swine, and the whole herd rushed down the steep bank into the sea where they drowned. [33]The swineherds ran away, and when they came to the town they reported everything, including what had happened to the demoniacs. [34]Thereupon the whole town came out to meet Jesus, and when they saw him they begged him to leave their district.

The next healing, an exorcism, is a bit strange. The two Gadarenes are possessed by demons (8:28-34). Matthew has a penchant for doubling characters in some stories (cf. Mk 5:1-20; also Mt 9:27-31). The setting is, for Matthew, Gentile territory; Jews associated pigs with Gentiles. The story shows how the demons recognize Jesus and beg him to send them into a local herd of swine rather than destroy them outright. Jesus had already shown his ability to defeat the devil, the tempter and prince of evil (4:1-11), but the devil's little minions keep bothering people. Paradoxically, Jesus' ability to exorcize demons eventually leads to the charge that he does miracles by that very power of evil (9:34). That is one of the problems with miracles—they can be interpreted one way or another. That does not keep Jesus from saving the demoniacs and driving out the demons. In this case, the reaction to Jesus is one of fear, for the townspeople ask him to depart. Confronting evil directly can be a frightening experience, especially if we don't under-stand the power that can dominate it.

$^{9:1}$ He entered a boat, made the crossing, and came into his own town. ^{2}And there people brought to him a paralytic lying on a stretcher. When Jesus saw their faith, he said to the paralytic, "Courage, child, your sins are forgiven." ^{3}At that, some of the scribes said to themselves, "This man is blaspheming." ^{4}Jesus knew what they were thinking, and said, "Why do you harbor evil thoughts? ^{5}Which is easier, to say, 'Your sins are forgiven,' or to say, 'Rise and walk'? ^{6}But that you may know that the Son of Man has authority on earth to forgive sins"—he then said to the paralytic, "Rise, pick up your stretcher, and go home." ^{7}He rose and went home. ^{8}When the crowds saw this they were struck with awe and glorified God who had given such authority to human beings.

The healing of a paralytic is the third miracle in this section (9:1-8). The focus in this story is that healing has two layers of meaning. Jesus has thus far shown that he can heal physically, that he can control the forces of nature, and that he can overpower demons. But something more sinister and debilitating lurks in the human psyche, sinfulness. Many people might agree that the guilt that accompanies recognition of sin can be very paralyzing. Modern science even indicates a connection between psychological/emotional health and physical health. Paralysis can take many forms. When Jesus' first response to the paralytic is to indicate that his sins are forgiven, it leads to the charge of blaspheming God, who according to Jewish tradition, had sole power to forgive sins. This, in turn, leads to Jesus' second response which is to heal the paralytic physically. The response of the crowd is to recognize the authority (*exousia,* 9:8; cf. 7:29; 28:18) God has given Jesus. Many people are as paralyzed by their own sense of guilt, fear, and insecurity as by serious physical disabilities. Jesus can unshackle whatever chains bind us in life.

^{9}As Jesus passed on from there, he saw a man named Matthew sitting at the customs post. He said to him, "Follow me." And he got up and followed him. ^{10}While he was at table in his house, many tax collectors and sinners came and sat with Jesus and his disciples. [11] The Pharisees saw this and said to his disciples, "Why does your teacher eat with tax collectors and sinners?" [12] He heard this and said, "Those who are well do not need a physician, but the sick do. [13] Go and learn the meaning of the words, 'I desire mercy, not sacrifice.' I did not come to call the righteous but sinners."

The miracles are again interrupted with a story about discipleship. The call of Matthew the tax collector (9:9-13) contrasts with the previous story of the would-be volunteers (8:18-22). Despite Matthew's outcast status as one who fed off of others' obligation to pay taxes, Jesus walks by and simply issues the command, "Follow me" (v. 9). Like the four initial disciples, Matthew's call takes place in the midst of his work. There is no discussion, no delay. Matthew did not enlist, but he heard the call and answered it immediately. Later, at table with Jesus and a group of sinners, the Pharisees complain to the disciples about Jesus attracting such a motley crew (vv. 10-11). Jesus' marvelous response that the sick need a doctor, not healthy people, demolishes the objection. He challenges them to return to the scriptures and interpret properly what Hosea meant by the words, "I desire mercy, not sacrifice" (v. 13, Hos 6:6). This is Jesus' way of saying that his enemies have their priorities confused. Worship is fine; it is important in the life of the community, but responding to people's needs takes precedence. I emphasize that this passage does not denigrate liturgical celebration. It only puts it in proper perspective.

The following passage continues the controversy in a different vein (9:14-17). When Jesus is asked by John the Baptist's disciples about why they do not observe the required fasting rules, he responds that you don't stop partying when the bridegroom is still around. More importantly, something new is happening that requires a new response. So Jesus recommends putting new wine into new wineskins. This image represents symbolically Matthew's struggle with how to cope with the

Judaism that has been dramatically changed by Jesus' coming. Although Jesus preserved the essentials of the Torah, his radicalizing of the Law exhibited in the Sermon on the Mount indicated that there was no turning back. Trying to dress up the old with cosmetic changes, when an interior conversion is what is needed, won't do. In the context of Jesus' miracles, this passage emphasizes that, in Jesus, God is accomplishing something wholly new, yet in continuity with his revealed Law.

Healing an Official's Daughter, a Woman with Hemorrhage and Two Other Miracles (9:18-34)

[18] While he was saying these things to them, an official came forward, knelt down before him, and said, "My daughter has just died. But come, lay your hand on her, and she will live." [19] Jesus rose and followed him, and so did his disciples. [20] A woman suffering hemorrhages for twelve years came up behind him and touched the tassel on his cloak. [21] She said to herself, "If only I can touch his cloak, I shall be cured." [22] Jesus turned around and saw her, and said, "Courage, daughter! Your faith has saved you." And from that hour the woman was cured. [23]

When Jesus arrived at the official's house and saw the flute players and the crowd who were making a commotion, [24] he said, "Go away! The girl is not dead but sleeping." And they ridiculed him. [25] When the crowd was put out, he came and took her by the hand, and the little girl arose. [26] And news of this spread throughout all that land.

These controversies give way to the final three miracle stories, one of which contains two miracle events (9:18-34). The first one recounts the story of some sort of "official" (he is Jewish in Mark 5:22) who intercedes on behalf of his sick daughter who, like the centurion's servant, is at a distance (9:18-26). Meanwhile, a woman suffering with a hemorrhage for twelve years seeks to be healed merely by touching Jesus' cloak. Jesus commends her faith and the healing is accomplished (v. 22). Upon arriving at the centurion's house, Jesus dismisses the premature mourners who have gathered and enters the house to heal the girl (v. 25). This is apparently an example of raising the dead. Although the text does not explicitly say the girl was dead, that is the implication. We could, of course, ask whether medically she was in a coma or a state of suspended animation, but that is not the point. Matthew sees here Jesus' ability to raise even the dead, something that he will experience himself in the resurrection and that will affect the lives of others (27:53; 28:6). Here again is a strong christological message in the miracle. In this miracle Jesus' healing power extends in two different directions. In the one, a woman reaches out and touches him; in the other, Jesus touches a little girl. Both are healing moments.

[27] And as Jesus passed on from there, two blind men followed (him), crying out, "Son of David, have pity on us!" [28] When he entered the house, the blind men approached him and Jesus said to them, "Do you believe that I can do this?" "Yes, Lord," they said to him. [29] Then he touched their eyes and said, "Let it be done for you according to your faith." [30] And their eyes were opened. Jesus warned them sternly, "See that no one knows about this." [31] But they went out and spread word of him through all that land.

[32] As they were going out, a demoniac who could not speak was brought to him, [33] and when the demon was driven out the mute person spoke. The crowds were amazed and said, "Nothing like this has ever been seen in Israel." [34] But the Pharisees said, "He drives out demons by the prince of demons."

[35] Jesus went around to all the towns and villages, teaching in their synagogues, proclaiming the gospel of the kingdom, and curing every disease and illness. [36] At the sight of the crowds, his heart was moved with pity for them because they were troubled and abandoned, like sheep without a shepherd. [37] Then he said to his disciples, "The harvest is abundant but

the laborers are few; [38]so ask the master of the harvest to send out laborers for his harvest."

The final two miracles, the healing of two blind men (9:27-31) and a mute person (9:32-34) continue the demonstration of Jesus' enormous power to heal. In the first instance, Jesus is addressed as Son of David, alluding to a Jewish understanding of Solomon's ability to heal. In response to the healing of the mute person the crowds again are amazed and claim that nothing like it has been experienced in Israel (v. 33). The snide comment of the Pharisees, however, attributing the power to the devil, shows that not everyone is convinced even by miracles. The entire section of miracle stories concludes with the summary passage we have already discussed and that provides a transition to the next major discourse of Jesus (9:35-38). Jesus shows himself to be a good shepherd watching over his needy flocks. But he warns that there is a lack of assistants to help with this ministry.

What is the effect of these miracle stories? There are two main themes that intersect in these stories. The first is christological. They confirm Jesus' messianic identity, power, and authority as God's Son. They prepare for the final confirmation on the cross where he will "prove" his identity even more forcefully by his surrender to his Father's will (27:45-54). The second is ecclesiological, seen by the presence of the digressions within the sets of miracles. Discipleship will not arise solely from witnessing miraculous and unexplainable deeds. Jesus' power is not used to force or trick people into discipleship. People must, rather, respond to a call because of their own encounter with him. They must hear the call and answer it freely.

The miracles also challenge us to honor God's ability to enter the human arena in ways that go beyond our understanding. Miracles are an acknowledgment that we are not the ones in absolute control of our lives. Faith urges us to place ourselves squarely in the Lord's care. We should acknowledge our neediness before God ("Lord, save us!" [cf. Mt 14:30]) and have confidence that God can accomplish even what seems impossible. Scientific research has been taking place that suggests that those with faith and a life of prayer stand a better chance of healing well in dire illnesses than those who have no religious leanings. Skeptics might attribute this to the power of mind over matter. From a faith perspective, it is simply placing ourselves in the hands of Jesus. It is a desire to touch him and be touched by him. Actively and passively, Jesus heals. Preoccupation with miracles is not a good thing, but neither is outright rejection of them. The gospel message places us in the middle of life, in the midst of our trials and tribulations, which is exactly where life is lived. This is precisely where Jesus desires to encounter us, for he came for sinners (9:13).

The Twelve Apostles (10:1-4)

[1] Then he summoned his twelve disciples and gave them authority over unclean spirits to drive them out and to cure every disease and every illness. [2] The names of the twelve apostles are these: first, Simon called Peter, and his brother Andrew; James, the son of Zebedee, and his brother John; [3] Philip and Bartholomew, Thomas and Matthew the tax collector; James, the son of Alphaeus, and Thaddeus; [4] Simon the Cananean, and Judas Iscariot who betrayed him.

After demonstrating in word and deed that he is God's chosen instrument, Jesus proceeds to share his healing power with his disciples and to instruct them in a second discourse more specifically about the challenges that await them (10:1–11:1).

The list of the twelve, representing the twelve tribes of Israel, is given without any narration as to when and how the others were called (10:2-4). The list is quite simple yet profound. Simon is listed "first" and we are told he is called "Peter," the name by which later tradition most readily remembers him. He is first in more ways than one, for the story will make it clear that he serves as the primary spokesman for his colleagues (16:16-19; 19:27; 26:33). The last one listed is Judas Iscariot, with the sorry epitaph "who betrayed him" (v. 4). In between is a group of ten men who, for the most part, have disappeared from history in all but legend. Little historical information remains of Jesus' original chosen ones. Legends abound, some with possible foundation but most with little assurance of historical accuracy. Yet the list provides some comfort to us. It tells us two things. First, following Jesus is not a path to fame and fortune. It may rather lead to obscurity. The fact that little information remains of the original twelve indicates that being remembered is of little value in fostering the kingdom of God. Second, the fact that some of these individuals either denied, betrayed, or deserted Jesus should provide us some assurance that even the great ones don't always pan out. We may be unworthy of Jesus in many facets, but that need not prevent us from taking the risk of joining him when we are invited. I doubt that we can do much worse than the original group. Nor do I think Jesus was a bad judge of character. On the contrary, he came to call sinners, not the righteous (9:13). So the list paradoxically contains a message of hope.

Instructions for the Disciples (10:5–11:1)

[5] Jesus sent out these twelve after instructing them thus,

"Do not go into pagan territory or enter a Samaritan town. [6] Go rather to the lost sheep of the house of Israel. [7] As you go, make this proclamation: 'The kingdom of heaven is at hand.' [8] Cure the sick, raise the dead, cleanse lepers, drive out demons. Without cost you have received; without cost you are to give. [9] Do not take gold or silver or copper for your belts; [10] no sack for the journey, or a second tunic, or sandals, or walking stick. The laborer deserves his keep.

[11] "Whatever town or village you enter, look for a worthy person in it, and stay there until you leave. [12] As you enter a

house, wish it peace. [13] If the house is worthy, let your peace come upon it; if not, let your peace return to you. [14] Whoever will not receive you or listen to your words—go outside that house or town and shake the dust from your feet. [15] Amen, I say to you, it will be more tolerable for the land of Sodom and Gomorrah on the day of judgment than for that town.

[16] "Behold, I am sending you like sheep in the midst of wolves; so be shrewd as serpents and simple as doves. [17] But beware of people, for they will hand you over to courts and scourge you in their synagogues, [18] and you will be led before governors and kings for my sake as a witness before them and the pagans. [19] When they hand you over, do not worry about how you are to speak or what you are to say. You will be given at that moment what you are to say. [20] For it will not be you who speak but the Spirit of your Father speaking through you. [21] "Brother will hand over brother to death, and the father his child; children will rise up against parents and have them put to death. [22] You will be hated by all because of my name, but whoever endures to the end will be saved. [23] When they persecute you in one town, flee to another. Amen, I say to you, you will not finish the towns of Israel before the Son of Man comes.

[24] "No disciple is above his teacher, no slave above his master. [25] It is enough for the disciple that he become like his teacher, for the slave that he become like his master. If they have called the master of the house Beelzebul, how much more those of his household! [26] Therefore do not be afraid of them. Nothing is concealed that will not be revealed, nor secret that will not be known. [27] What I say to you in the darkness, speak in the light; what you hear whispered, proclaim on the housetops.

[28] "And do not be afraid of those who kill the body but cannot kill the soul; rather, be afraid of the one who can destroy both soul and body in Gehenna. [29] Are not two sparrows sold for a small coin? Yet not one of them falls to the ground without your Father's knowledge. [30] Even all the hairs of your head are counted. [31] So do not be afraid; you are worth more than many sparrows. [32] Everyone who acknowledges me

before others I will acknowledge before my heavenly Father. [33] But whoever denies me before others, I will deny before my heavenly Father.

[34] "Do not think that I have come to bring peace upon the earth. I have come to bring not peace but the sword. [35] For I have come to set a man against his father, a daughter against her mother, and a daughter-in-law against her mother-in-law; [36] and one's enemies will be those of his household.

[37] "Whoever loves father or mother more than me is not worthy of me, and whoever loves son or daughter more than me is not worthy of me; [38] and whoever does not take up his cross and follow after me is not worthy of me. [39] Whoever finds his life will lose it, and whoever loses his life for my sake will find it.

[40] "Whoever receives you receives me, and whoever receives me receives the one who sent me. [41] Whoever receives a prophet because he is a prophet will receive a prophet's reward, and whoever receives a righteous man because he is righteous will receive a righteous man's reward. [42] And whoever gives only a cup of cold water to one of these little ones to drink because he is a disciple—amen, I say to you, he will surely not lose his reward."

[11:1] When Jesus finished giving these commands to his twelve disciples, he went away from that place to teach and to preach in their towns.

This discourse lays out the parameters of the disciples' ministry as they are sent out to preach and heal. One notices that they are not instructed yet to teach; that will come later after the resurrection (28:19-20). But they are given a full share in Jesus' power and authority (10:1,8), and they preach the exact same message as Jesus and John the Baptist before him: "The kingdom of heaven is at hand" (10:7; cf. 3:1; 4:17). Jesus' instruction can be summarized and paraphrased through a kind of checklist of important reminders.

1) don't go anywhere but Israel (vv. 5-6); a worldwide mission is later (28:18-20)
2) don't take anything extra with you because of the urgency of the message (vv. 9-10)
3) accept whatever hospitality is offered in return for your ministry (vv. 11-13)
4) wherever you go, bring peace to those you meet (v. 12)
5) don't waste time trying to convince those who won't accept your message but move on to the next town (v. 14)
6) get ready to suffer for the sake of the message you bear (vv. 16-25)
7) regardless of what persecution you face, don't be afraid, for God will provide what you need to survive (vv. 26-33)
8) be prepared to abandon even your own family for the sake of the gospel (v. 37)
9) get ready to bear your own cross and follow after Jesus (v. 38)
10) remember that whoever receives you receives Jesus and thus receives the one who sent him (v. 40)
11) have hope in the reward that awaits your faithfulness to the mission, a reward tantamount to the prophets and the righteous of old (vv. 41-42).

Such a list of exhortations is too quick a summation to do the instruction justice, yet we get a sense of the urgency and practicality of Jesus' discourse. The discourse seems to go in three different directions at once. One path reviews the purpose, urgency, and power of the mission. It describes the need to heal, to preach, and to go from town to town spreading the good news of the kingdom. In this ministry the disciples are imitating Jesus who, in turn, supports them (vv. 23-25). Another path reviews the pitfalls that will accompany this journey. Persecution, being hauled into court and before religious and civil authorities may almost seem mild compared to the warning that families will themselves be split up over this mission (vv. 21,34-36). The gospel message paradoxically results in hatred and lack of peace (vv. 22,34). The final path provides an assurance that, despite the severe difficulties that will arise, God will provide the words to speak in defense (v. 19) and a reward for all that is suffered (vv. 28-32,41-42) because we are worth more than the littlest creatures whom God protects (vv. 30-31).

Discipleship is like the convergence of these three paths. The disciples are the "little ones" (v. 42) who should be well received but who will often become the refuse of the world. Jesus also likens them to sheep sent in the midst of wolves (v. 16), hardly a comforting thought. Trying to be light in a dark world is not easy (v. 27). If people have accused the master of working for the devil (v. 25), how much quicker will they level the charge against his followers. Discipleship then and now has always been a risk. In chapter 10, Jesus lays out that risk in all its gory detail. Jesus gives the discourse ostensibly to the twelve, but the readers are transparently brought into the instruction as colleagues. If the risk gives us pause, it should. However, reconnoitering the landscape before we plunge into enemy territory is not cowardice but good sense. Coming on the heels of the miracles, Jesus' words remind us that discipleship is not always glorious. With the warning being clearly sounded in frank detail, Jesus sets out again to teach and preach (11:1; the third formulaic verse that concludes a discourse) and to confront the opposition that awaits. I suggest that you sit awhile with this discourse and let the words sink deeply into your own consciousness. They are timeless instructions not too difficult to grasp yet profound in their depth.

IV

Growing Opposition to Jesus
and his Disciples
(11:2–16:20)

The next section of the Gospel takes a turn into opposition
territory in a way that goes beyond the premonitions that have
thus far been given in the story (11:2–12:50). Controversy
takes center stage in this part of the Gospel and prepares for an
escalation that will carry the story to its inevitable conclusion.

Chapter eleven consists of three main divisions. The first
concerns John the Baptist (11:2-19). The second is a reproach
to the unrepentant cities of Galilee (11:20-24). The third is a
prayer of thanksgiving that exalts Jesus' special relationship to
his heavenly Father (11:25-30).

John the Baptist (11:2-19)

[2] When John heard in prison of the works of the Messiah,
he sent his disciples to him [3] with this question, "Are you the
one who is to come, or should we look for another?" [4] Jesus
said to them in reply, "Go and tell John what you hear and
see: [5] the blind regain their sight, the lame walk, lepers are
cleansed, the deaf hear, the dead are raised, and the poor have
the good news proclaimed to them. [6] And blessed is the one
who takes no offense at me."

[7] As they were going off, Jesus began to speak to the crowds
about John, "What did you go out to the desert to see? A reed
swayed by the wind? [8] Then what did you go out to see?
Someone dressed in fine clothing? Those who wear fine
clothing are in royal palaces. [9] Then why did you go out? To

see a prophet? Yes, I tell you, and more than a prophet. [10]This is the one about whom it is written:

'Behold, I am sending my messenger ahead of you;
he will prepare your way before you.'

[11] "Amen, I say to you, among those born of women there has been none greater than John the Baptist; yet the least in the kingdom of heaven is greater than he. [12]From the days of John the Baptist until now, the kingdom of heaven suffers violence, and the violent are taking it by force. [13] All the prophets and the law prophesied up to the time of John. [14]And if you are willing to accept it, he is Elijah, the one who is to come. [15] Whoever has ears ought to hear.

[16] "To what shall I compare this generation? It is like children who sit in marketplaces and call to one another, [17]'We played the flute for you, but you did not dance, we sang a dirge but you did not mourn.'

[18] "For John came neither eating nor drinking, and they said, 'He is possessed by a demon.' [19]The Son of Man came eating and drinking and they said, 'Look, he is a glutton and a drunkard, a friend of tax collectors and sinners.' But wisdom is vindicated by her works."

John the Baptist is a figure that reappears at this juncture of the story because he has heard in prison about the works that Jesus has performed (11:2). Jesus' reputation entices John's curiosity. Just who is this Jesus? John sends messengers with the question, and Jesus responds by telling the messengers to report what they have heard and seen. The works of Jesus, of course, are astounding. The blind can see, the lame walk, lepers are cleansed, deaf people hear, the poor receive hopeful news, and even the dead are raised to life (v. 5). In other words, Jesus' deeds indicate a fulfillment of the prophetic hope expressed most explicitly by Isaiah the prophet (Is 35:5-6; 61:1). They suggest that God's reign has come in the person of Jesus, for he performs the works of the messiah. The evidence directly confronts John's question, "Are you the one who is to come, or should we look for another?" (v. 3) Jesus adds, "And blessed is the one who takes no offense at me" (v. 6). The verb "take offense" or "stumble" (*skandalizomai*) is important in this context. It characterizes exactly the nature of the opposition Jesus encounters in these chapters and the rest of the story (cf. 13:57; 15:12; 17:27). The religious leaders are scandalized at the words and deeds of Jesus. The root meaning of the verb, however, is to cause others to stumble. Their attitude can negatively affect others. John the Baptist proffers an honest question, but it gives the opportunity for Jesus to praise John's own role in the drama of salvation history (11:7-19).

Basically, John is praised for his asceticism and his preparation for Jesus' own coming. Matthew makes explicit that John is none other than Elijah, the prophet of the end time who was taken up to heaven in a fiery chariot and who was to return only in the days prior to the messiah (see 2 Kgs 2:11-12). Jesus then says that, unfortunately, "this generation," the pejorative term for stubborn Israel (12:39-42,45; 16:4; 17:17; 23:36; 24:34), was too fickle to accept either John in his ascetic mode or Jesus in his bolder profile (vv. 17-19). The people of Israel are like spoiled children who can't make up their mind what they want to do. As worthy as John is in his background role, Jesus states just how new the kingdom is that he is bringing: "yet the least in the kingdom of heaven is greater than he" (v. 11). John straddles both worlds in a sense. He is associated with the prophets of the OT by the violence that occasionally befell them (the allusion to violence in the mysterious verse 12). He prepared well for Jesus' coming, yet he does not belong to the new kingdom; neither does he belong to the OT era. Matthew's Jesus seems to indicate that the law and prophets no longer have the same weight as before, now that the gospel message has arrived. Curiously, the usual expression "the law and prophets" is reversed in verse 13 ("all the prophets and the law"). The reason is that all of Jesus' ministry, especially his fate, comes under the direction of the prophetic scriptures which will take him to his death (26:56). From this perspective, the prophetic word has taken precedence in Jesus' ministry and even over-shadowed the Law.

The Impenitent Towns (11:20-24)

[20] Then he began to reproach the towns where most of his mighty deeds had been done, since they had not repented. [21] "Woe to you, Chorazin! Woe to you, Bethsaida! For if the mighty deeds done in your midst had been done in Tyre and Sidon, they would long ago have repented in sackcloth and ashes. [22] But I tell you, it will be more tolerable for Tyre and Sidon on the day of judgment than for you. [23] And as for you, Capernaum:

'Will you be exalted to heaven?
You will go down to the netherworld.'

For if the mighty deeds done in your midst had been done in Sodom, it would have remained until this day. [24] But I tell you, it will be more tolerable for the land of Sodom on the day of judgment than for you."

The reproaches against Chorazin, Bethsaida and Capernaum, three towns of Galilee, show Jesus' justifiable anger with the stubbornness of his own people who fail to accept him (11:20-24). So serious is their rejection that they are compared to the legendary towns of Tyre, Sidon, and Sodom, cities denounced in the OT for their evil. Galilee's cities will suffer worse consequences for their rejection of Jesus. Even Jesus' mighty deeds are not enough to convince them. In their obstinacy they reinforce the ironic fact that those who should be most open to hearing the message are not. "Whoever has ears ought to hear" (11:15), Jesus says, but too often people hear what they want to hear rather than the truth.

Praise of the Father and the Gentle Wisdom of the Son (11:25-30)

[25] At that time Jesus said in reply, "I give praise to you, Father, Lord of heaven and earth, for although you have hidden these things from the wise and the learned you have revealed them to the childlike. [26] Yes, Father, such has been your gracious will. [27] All things have been handed over to me by my Father. No one knows the Son except the Father, and no one knows the Father except the Son and anyone to whom the Son wishes to reveal him.

[28] "Come to me, all you who labor and are burdened, and I will give you rest. [29] Take my yoke upon you and learn from me, for I am meek and humble of heart; and you will find rest for yourselves. [30] For my yoke is easy, and my burden light."

Finally, Jesus turns to praise of his Father. The "childlike" (=disciples) have received God's revelation in Jesus rather than the "wise and learned" (=Israel's leaders). In a passage that seems more at home in the Gospel of John than here, Jesus speaks in poignant terms of the closeness of his Father. This is the source of his power and authority (11:27; cf. 28:18). Throughout Matthew's Gospel the close relationship between Jesus and his heavenly Father is apparent (7:21; 10:32-33; 11:27, etc.). Matthew, more than Mark or Luke, refers respectfully to God as Father. This relationship does not "go to Jesus' head," however, but leads him to a deeper, more compassionate ministry. Echoing Lady Wisdom from the OT, Jesus' next words extend an open invitation for all who are burdened by life's hardships to come to him (11:28-30; cf. Sir 51:26-27). These tender words have provided generations of Christians with comfort in times of difficulty. Christian preachers have often noted that Jesus has broad shoulders. He can take on whatever burdens we care to dump on him. That he is "meek and humble of heart" also reminds us what Jesus taught as an attitude reflective of God's kingdom (5:5; cf. 21:5). He will continually demonstrate that he is the meek, lowly servant, a humble messiah (21:5). In contrast to the religious leaders who oppose him and who lay "heavy burdens" on others (23:4), Jesus' burden is light (v. 30). Even when confronted with opposition, Jesus gets his own priorities straight. He is about his Father's business and nothing will detract him from that mission, even if some will not accept him.

Controversy (12:1-21)

[1] At that time Jesus was going through a field of grain on the sabbath. His disciples were hungry and began to pick the heads of grain and eat them. [2] When the Pharisees saw this, they said to him, "See, your disciples are doing what is unlawful to do on the sabbath." [3] He said to them, "Have you not read what David did when he and his companions were hungry, [4] how he went into the house of God and ate the bread of offering, which neither he nor his companions but only the priests could lawfully eat? [5] Or have you not read in the law that on the sabbath the priests serving in the temple violate the sabbath and are innocent? [6] I say to you, something greater than the temple is here. [7] If you knew what this meant, 'I desire mercy, not sacrifice,' you would not have condemned these innocent men. [8] For the Son of Man is Lord of the sabbath."

Chapter twelve portrays the escalation of opposition to Jesus with a series of controversies over Jesus' actions. It contains five parts. The first part describes Jesus performing two actions that provoke his enemies (12:1-14). The first action occurs when Jesus' disciples walk through a field on the sabbath and in hunger pick grain to eat (12:1-8). The action violates the sabbath law as a day of rest. The Pharisees question Jesus' permissiveness, to which he responds with words that imply they are in the presence of something greater than the Temple and all its laws. Jesus uses an example from David's life in the OT to illustrate that in the Davidic tradition in which he stands, he can dispense with the customary legal obligation (see 1 Sm

21:2-6). Moreover, Jesus says, the real reason is that "the Son of Man is Lord of the Sabbath" (v. 8). He sends his opponents back to the scriptures to learn the meaning of Hosea's plea for mercy not sacrifice (Hos 6:6; cf. Mt 9:13). In essence, Jesus rebukes his opposition because they are in the presence of a greater power they do not recognize. The real question is, where should the priority lie? Sabbath rules are fine in their proper place, but they do not take precedence in light of the greater authority of Jesus.

> [9] Moving on from there, he went into their synagogue. [10] And behold, there was a man there who had a withered hand. They questioned him, "Is it lawful to cure on the sabbath?" so that they might accuse him. [11] He said to them, "Which one of you who has a sheep that falls into a pit on the sabbath will not take hold of it and lift it out? [12] How much more valuable a person is than a sheep. So it is lawful to do good on the sabbath." [13] Then he said to the man, "Stretch out your hand." He stretched it out, and it was restored as sound as the other. [14] But the Pharisees went out and took counsel against him to put him to death. [15] When Jesus realized this, he withdrew from that place. Many (people) followed him, and he cured them all, [16] but he warned them not to make him known.

The second controversy involves Jesus' authority to heal on the sabbath. In the presence of a man with a withered hand in their synagogue on the same day, they ask Jesus whether it is lawful to heal on the sabbath (12:9-14). Jesus responds with a story about a sheep that falls into a pit. If a person would seek to pull it out on the sabbath, how much more valuable is it to heal a human being on that day? He then proceeds to heal the man, and the Pharisees begin to plot Jesus' death (12:14). This is a fatal escalation in the struggle. Jesus' opponents now put into motion a plot foreseen in the infancy narrative and that will wind its way to the cross ("took counsel against"; cf. 22:15; 27:1,7; 28:12). The Pharisees come across looking like hopelessly obtuse individuals who are so fixated on their enemy that they are blind to their own failings. They do not recognize the greater authority in their midst. Rather than rejoice at a healing, they brood over Jesus' apparent violation of the Law.

We need a word about Pharisees here. Actually, from an historical standpoint, the Pharisees were an outstanding group of lay people who sought to make the Jewish Law more livable by allowing for oral interpretation as well as the written code. By Matthew's time, however, the Pharisees were the only formal group to have survived the destruction of Jerusalem in AD 70. They were probably neighbors to the Matthean community. When the followers of Jesus, however, pushed the implications of Jesus' message to its final goal, the relationship between the groups broke down. "Pharisee" became equated with the stubborn, legalistic, hypocritical establishment that could not cope with change. The tendency we must avoid is to make the Pharisees the essence of hypocrisy as regards the Jews. Historically, they were not, but some of them may have been involved in plotting against Jesus along with some other Jewish leaders. What Matthew does here is make them the prime initiators in the plot because in his day they were the only visible Jews. Interestingly, the passion narrative itself mentions the Pharisees only once (27:62). Instead, the chief priests, scribes, and elders of the people are the main actors opposing Jesus. I think the more important issue is to direct the passage's interpretation inwardly. Do we allow our own religion to so calcify as to be unadaptable when God's values confront our human preferences? Religious people of any stripe are likely candidates to fall into hypocrisy. The Greek notion (*hypokrisis*), of course, comes from the world of theater where people wore masks to portray various emotions. A constant danger in most religions is to masquerade our piety when our attitudes or actions are otherwise.

In light of this opposition Jesus withdraws and a summary passage describes his ongoing ministry of healing (12:15-16). Matthew frequently uses the word "withdrew" (*anachoreo*) in such contexts of opposition (cf. 2:14,22; 4:12; 14:13; 15:21); Jesus' time has not come yet (8:29; 26:2,45). The scene is coupled with another fulfillment citation from Isaiah the prophet (12:17-21) from a section devoted to the Suffering Servant (Is 42:1-4). The effect is twofold. It identifies Jesus as God's servant who will suffer for his ministry, and in spite of it, the Gentiles will be the beneficiaries because they will receive justice and hope (12:18,21). The double mention of the Gentiles in this passage points to the irony of the controversies surrounding Jesus. His own people will reject him, but outsiders will receive him.

Further Opposition to Jesus (12:22-45)

²²Then they brought to him a demoniac who was blind and mute. He cured the mute person so that he could speak and see. ²³ All the crowd was astounded, and said, "Could this perhaps be the Son of David?" ²⁴ But when the Pharisees heard this, they said, "This man drives out demons only by the power of Beelzebul, the prince of demons." ²⁵But he knew what they were thinking and said to them, "Every kingdom divided against itself will be laid waste, and no town or house divided against itself will stand. ²⁶ And if Satan drives out Satan, he is divided against himself; how, then, will his kingdom stand? ²⁷And if I drive out demons by Beelzebul, by whom do your own people drive them out? Therefore they will be your judges. ²⁸ But if it is by the Spirit of God that I drive out demons, then the kingdom of God has come upon you. ²⁹How can anyone enter a strong man's house and steal his property, unless he first ties up the strong man? Then he can plunder his house. ³⁰ Whoever is not with me is against me, and whoever does not gather with me scatters. ³¹ Therefore, I say to you, every sin and blasphemy will be forgiven people, but blasphemy against the Spirit will not be forgiven. ³²And whoever speaks a word against the Son of Man will be forgiven; but whoever speaks against the holy Spirit will not be forgiven, either in this age or in the age to come."

The opposition does not deter Jesus. The next section of the Gospel (12:22-50) continues with another healing story that offers Jesus a chance to expound further on "this generation" and its failures. The cure of the person who is both blind and mute (v. 22) leads to four teachings. The first one is that a divided kingdom cannot stand (vv. 24-32). Jesus' accusers claim that he works for Satan, Beelzebul, but if that were so, how could Satan's kingdom possibly survive with an insider casting out demons? Jesus instead talks about sin and forgiveness in the context of the choice that must be made. We are either for or against Jesus (v. 30). There is no neutrality or bargaining; one cannot straddle the fence with Jesus. Any sin can be forgiven except "blasphemy against the Spirit" (v. 31). This mysterious saying has caused no end of trouble for interpreters through the ages. It appears to limit God's grace. In this context, however, it is tied to the Jewish leaders' accusation that Jesus is in league with Satan. The sin against the Spirit is likely the failure to believe the "good news" that in Jesus' ministry God's kingdom has indeed come upon us (v. 28), and instead falsely to attribute to Satan's doing what is actually God's. The one unforgivable sin is the inability to hope in God's power to accomplish this miraculous ministry.

> [33] "Either declare the tree good and its fruit is good, or declare the tree rotten and its fruit is rotten, for a tree is known by its fruit. [34] You brood of vipers, how can you say good things when you are evil? For from the fullness of the heart the mouth speaks. [35] A good person brings forth good out of a store of goodness, but an evil person brings forth evil out of a store of evil. [36] I tell you, on the day of judgment people will render an account for every careless word they speak. [37] By your words you will be acquitted, and by your words you will be condemned."

The second teaching rekindles an image that Jesus had used in the Sermon on the Mount. Good trees bear good fruit, and bad trees bear bad fruit (12:37; cf. 7:15-20). Here again Jesus is focusing on what is really essential in faith. One's deeds reflect one's interior attitude. The inside and outside correspond whether we admit it or not. Jesus also emphasizes that the very words we speak can give us away, for words express what the heart holds dear (v. 34). Word and deed can never be far apart in the proclamation of the gospel. Have you ever spoken a word you wished you hadn't? Perhaps an insult, an unkind remark, a premature judgment. Once spoken, words have a life of their own. Here Jesus calls us to greater caution in our language.

> [38] Then some of the scribes and Pharisees said to him, "Teacher, we wish to see a sign from you." [39] He said to them in reply, "An evil and unfaithful generation seeks a sign, but no sign will be given it except the sign of Jonah the prophet. [40] Just as Jonah was in the belly of the whale three days and three nights, so will the Son of Man be in the heart of the earth three days and three nights. [41] At the judgment, the men of Nineveh will arise with this generation and condemn it, because they repented at the preaching of Jonah; and there is something greater than Jonah here. [42] At the judgment the queen of the south will arise with this generation and condemn it, because she came from the ends of the earth to hear the wisdom of Solomon; and there is something greater than Solomon here."

The third teaching in this section comes in response to a request from the scribes and Pharisees for a sign (12:38-42). Jesus' reference to "an evil and unfaithful generation" is representative of his judgment about the religious leadership of his day. Before they believe, they want proof. They are seeking an insurance policy, a sign, that Jesus is who he seems to be. Sadly, the desire for signs is an ever-present danger to faith. Many today still seek signs. But faith by its very nature is trusting in God. It does not have a built-in security blanket. The only sign Jesus assents to is "the sign of Jonah the prophet" (v. 40). Everyone knows the story of this OT figure. Jonah tried to flee

God's command to go preach repentance to Israel's enemy, symbolized by the capital city of Nineveh (see the OT Book of Jonah). In the end, God derailed his attempted flight and he had to go to Nineveh to preach repentance. To Jonah's surprise, the Ninevites repented and God's destruction did not come upon them. Matthew's Jesus uses this story here to call forth repentance from those who stubbornly refuse to believe that God's kingdom is present in Jesus' words and deeds. Here is one greater than Jonah's preaching, greater than Solomon's wisdom, and still they want proof. Only repentance can bring them into the kingdom, a consistent message of John the Baptist and Jesus (3:2,8,11; 4:17).

> [43] "When an unclean spirit goes out of a person it roams through arid regions searching for rest but finds none. [44]Then it says, 'I will return to my home from which I came.' But upon returning, it finds it empty, swept clean, and put in order. [45] Then it goes and brings back with itself seven other spirits more evil than itself, and they move in and dwell there; and the last condition of that person is worse than the first. Thus it will be with this evil generation."

The final teaching (12:43-45) contains a warning about where "this generation's" stubbornness will lead. Like an unclean spirit that goes and gets seven more (the perfect number in the Bible) that are even more debased than itself, so will this "evil generation" end up worse than when they started. Evil has a way of multiplying itself. Resistance to repentance, the inability to read the signs that are right before our eyes, the excessive need to have every doubt erased before we will dare believe, all of these stand as stumbling blocks to faith. These four teachings in the context of controversy and opposition lead to the chapter's conclusion.

The True Family of Jesus (12:46-50)

⁴⁶While he was still speaking to the crowds, his mother and his brothers appeared outside, wishing to speak with him. ⁴⁷ [Someone told him, "Your mother and your brothers are standing outside, asking to speak with you."] ⁴⁸But he said in reply to the one who told him, "Who is my mother? Who are my brothers?" ⁴⁹And stretching out his hand toward his disciples, he said, "Here are my mother and my brothers. ⁵⁰ For whoever does the will of my heavenly Father is my brother, and sister, and mother."

Jesus' mother and brothers arrive on the scene seeking him (12:46-50). Upon hearing this, Jesus asks for the real identity of his relatives and replies, "For whoever does the will of my heavenly Father is my brother, and sister, and mother" (v. 50). Genetic relationship is not what the kingdom of God is about, nor does it involve being born into a family of faith. The genuine criterion for belonging to Jesus' new family, the family of disciples gathered around the one Father who is in heaven, is doing God's will. This punch line harks back to the failure of Jesus' opponents to bear good fruit (12:34-35). Jesus goes so far as to call them a "brood of vipers" (12:34; cf. 3:7; 23:33). They refuse to become part of the family Jesus is gathering because, in their very bones, they incarnate evil. It is a sad judgment to make, but the good news is that there are those who choose to follow Jesus. They become heralds of the kingdom, and the next section of the Gospel is devoted to giving them a glimpse in parabolic form of the kingdom that they are to proclaim.

Chapter thirteen is the parable chapter (13:1-53). It is the third of the five great discourses in Matthew, and it roughly parallels a similar chapter in Mark (4:1-33). A parable is a short, pithy image or story used to illustrate a deeper message. Most parables are similes (using the expression "like"), but some may be allegories (stories containing one-to-one correspondences with another reality). Matthew has a tendency for allegorizing parables, even though some may have been originally allegories, and he simply records them as such. The greatest temptation to interpreting parables is to reduce them only to stories with a moral. This, however, is not the best way to interpret parables. They are not simply concise sayings of moralistic wisdom. In Matthew parables are a glimpse of the kingdom of heaven. They are a window into God's way of viewing reality. In consequence, parables often tell us more about God and God's values than about ourselves, although we may find ourselves referenced in them. Since the parables are well known, I shall limit my presentation of scripture to one example and Jesus' explanation of the parables.

The Parable of the Sower and the Seed (13:1-9)

[1] On that day, Jesus went out of the house and sat down by the sea. [2] Such large crowds gathered around him that he got into a boat and sat down, and the whole crowd stood along the shore. [3] And he spoke to them at length in parables, saying: "A sower went out to sow. [4] And as he sowed, some seed fell on the path, and birds came and ate it up. [5] Some fell on rocky ground, where it had little soil. It sprang up at once because the soil was not deep, [6] and when the sun rose it was scorched, and it withered for lack of roots. [7] Some seed fell among thorns, and the thorns grew up and choked it. [8] But some seed fell on rich soil, and produced fruit, a hundred or sixty or thirtyfold. [9] Whoever has ears ought to hear."

The first and most paradigmatic parable is the famous parable of the sower (13:3-9). It is one of two parables that have their own built-in allegorical interpretation (13:18-23). Jesus speaks of seed that a sower sows, only to find that some falls on rocky ground or thorns and does not flourish, while some falls on rich soil. Jesus explains the meaning of the parable by emphasizing not the sower, but the seed and what happens to it. The seed represents four different kinds of hearers of God's Word. One kind hears "the word of the kingdom without understanding it," and so they are easily led astray by evil (13:19). Another kind hears the word but has no real rootedness to endure troubles or persecution, and so they also fall away (13:21). Yet another kind is led astray by worldly anxieties and the lure of wealth and success, and they do not endure either (13:22). A final kind hears the word and flourishes (13:23) leading to the conclusion that the seed will bear fruit in amounts of "a hundred or sixty or thirtyfold" (13:8,23).

As with many parables the symbolism is somewhat flexible. In the first version the seed would seemingly represent God's Word, but in the interpretation the seed becomes symbolic of various types of people who hear the Word. Most important, however, is to understand the decreasing harvest. It is contrary to what we would expect, especially because the seed in both narrations of the parable is described in increasing fashion (path → rocky ground → thorns → rich soil). How difficult it must have been for the Matthean community to recognize that even their efforts to sow the seed were not producing quite the results anticipated. Like some investors in the stock market, we might be sorely disappointed at our yield, come harvest time. Jesus' description acknowledges the possibility of low productivity. Yet it should not discourage us. Most important is to see that seed is sown. The rest is up to God. Even a low yield can please God.

This same perspective is reinforced by several other parables. The parable of the mustard seed (13:31-32) and the parable of the yeast (13:33) both speak of the miraculous way in which something mysteriously happens to cause growth. The tiny seed becomes a large tree, the batch of dough becomes leavened bread. In both instances unseen forces are at work to assure that the growth occurs. God's grace does that with the kingdom. In these instances *we* are not the force that produces the harvest. God does it, and that is how the kingdom can be slowly at work in our midst even if we do not always recognize it.

Another parable presents a tangential teaching, the parable of the tares or the weeds among the wheat (13:24-30). This parable also contains its own allegorical interpretation (13:36-43). Jesus likens the kingdom of heaven to a man who sowed good seed in his field, only to have an enemy secretly sow weeds in the same field. Any good farmer (or gardener) would go out and pull up the weeds so as not to lose much of the crop. But the man in the parable advises against that course of action. Rather, the weeds are allowed to grow alongside the wheat until harvest time when the wheat will be bundled and saved and the weeds bundled to burn. Jesus' explanation reveals that the "harvest" is the end time, the harvesters are God's angels, and the weeds are those who "cause others to sin and all evildoers" (v. 41). They will be thrown into the eternal fires of suffering but the righteous (=good seed) "will shine like the sun in the kingdom of their Father" (v. 43).

A similar note is sounded in the parable of the fish (13:47-50). The kingdom of God is compared to a net that catches fish of every kind that need to be sorted between good and bad. The good are preserved, the bad get thrown out into "the fiery furnace where there will be wailing and grinding of teeth" (v. 50), imagery connected with the suffering on judgment day (cf. 8:12; 13:42; 22:13; 24:51; 25:30). In both of these cases, the separation of good from bad, righteous from unrighteous, is crucial. But note the timing. It happens at the end time, the time of eschatological woe reminiscent of some of the OT prophets who warned of a day of judgment (Am 3:14; Zep 1:14-16). Yet in the case of the weed and wheat, the fact that the farmer allows them to grow side by side until harvest indicates that the separation is not something to be done right away. Many scholars think these parables mirror the situation in the Matthean community. Troubled by the presence of some evildoers, those who would lead others astray, there may have been an urge to cut them out, like some cancer, and throw them away. This is a human tendency. We want to set things right immediately. We have little patience to wait for God's own time of judgment. Matthew's community had apparently been involved in disconcerting relationships, especially with fellow

Jews and with some members of the community who were trou-
blesome (10:36; 18:15-17). But Jesus' parables recommend a
patient response to the presence of those in our midst who
cause difficulty. There will come a day of reckoning, but God's
kingdom will arrive to take care of that matter, and we are not
advised to take it into our own hands.

A final set of parables reveals another aspect of God's
kingdom. The twin parables of the treasure in the field and the
pearl of great price (13:44-46) both indicate that the kingdom
is so precious that one should be willing to sell everything in
order to possess it. Abandoning all in order to be utterly
devoted to God's kingdom is the ultimate challenge of discipleship. In these two parables Jesus lays out a model for our
behavior: risk everything in order to possess God's precious
kingdom. This would not normally be sound business advice.
How many people have "lost their shirt" in an investment
scheme that promised more than it could deliver? The kingdom
of heaven, however, is not a swindle. It is worth the risk.

The Reason for Parables (13:10-17)

[10] The disciples approached him and said, "Why do you
speak to them in parables?" [11] He said to them in reply,
"Because knowledge of the mysteries of the kingdom of
heaven has been granted to you, but to them it has not been
granted. [12] To anyone who has, more will be given and he will
grow rich; from anyone who has not, even what he has will be
taken away. [13] This is why I speak to them in parables,
because 'they look but do not see and hear but do not listen or
understand.' [14] Isaiah's prophecy is fulfilled in them, which
says:

'You shall indeed hear but not understand
you shall indeed look but never see.
[15] Gross is the heart of this people,
they will hardly hear with their ears,
they have closed their eyes,

lest they see with their eyes
and hear with their ears
and understand with their heart and be converted,
and I heal them.'
[16] "But blessed are your eyes, because they see, and your ears, because they hear. [17] Amen, I say to you, many prophets and righteous people longed to see what you see but did not see it, and to hear what you hear but did not hear it."

Tied to the parables is a passage that explains the logic of Jesus' parabolic teaching (13:10-17). Jesus clarifies that parables have two purposes. One is to present the kingdom to outsiders in a way that confuses them, and the other is to present the kingdom to the disciples, the insiders, in ways that reveal just how God operates. The disciples are incredibly privileged to receive this revelation. In typically prophetic fashion, and quoting another fulfillment citation from Isaiah (Is 6:9-10), Jesus explains that Israel does not receive his message because of their traditional stubbornness and hardness of heart. The parables make no sense to outsiders because they fail to have ears to hear and eyes to see (13:9,13-15,17). They miss the obvious. The disciples, on the other hand, are blessed even beyond the prophets and the sages to see and hear what heaven reveals (v. 17). The little ones have been blessed with revelation while the wise ones are kept in the dark (11:25). Discipleship brings us into close contact with the kingdom. The parables help us glimpse God's very will in action.

The section on parables concludes with the disciples' assent that they have understood Jesus' teaching. Jesus then pronounces that "every scribe who has been instructed in the kingdom of heaven is like the head of a house who brings from his storeroom both the new and the old" (13:52). This line seems to fit the evangelist perfectly. Some scholars see it as a subtle self-reference to the evangelist. Note the order, new and old. The new (=the gospel) takes precedence, yet the old (=the Law and the prophets) is still useful. Our own "storehouse" should have room for both new and old insights as well. Matthew is the master of combining traditions from the OT with Jesus' teaching, and he provides a good model. An image from the Middle Ages illustrates this insight well. In the famous cathedral at Chartres, France, is a remarkable stained glass window showing the four evangelists sitting on the shoulders of four OT prophets. The evangelists can see farther but only because they are sitting on the foundation of those who preceded them.

Jesus at Nazareth (13:54-58)

[54] He came to his native place and taught the people in their synagogue. They were astonished and said, "Where did this man get such wisdom and mighty deeds? [55] Is he not the carpenter's son? Is not his mother named Mary and his brothers James, Joseph, Simon, and Judas? [56] Are not his sisters all with us? Where did this man get all this?" [57] And they took offense at him. But Jesus said to them, "A prophet is not without honor except in his native place and in his own house." [58] And he did not work many mighty deeds there because of their lack of faith.

The next scene reinforces that Jesus' identity is still mysterious despite his great deeds and wonderful words (13:54-58). In his own native place of Nazareth Jesus' teaching and deeds cause astonishment and, in the end, offense. They, too, reject him. Jesus responds with a common prophetic explanation and a refusal to do many miracles because of their lack of faith. Prophets are unacceptable in their own home region (v. 57). This saying has become so commonplace that few doubt its truth, even in general terms. Preaching to one's own family and relatives is tricky business. Avoiding self-righteousness when trying to be righteous is difficult. Those closest to us know our foibles and our shortcomings. This makes it hard to be an effective evangelist to our own relatives and friends. Jesus' example indicates that no one is immune. It also reemphasizes the irony of his rejection by his own.

Chapters fourteen and fifteen are largely devoted to more of Jesus' miracle stories. Interspersed are passages about John the Baptist and further controversy with the Jewish leaders. In this section Jesus' image as a compassionate wonder-worker and authentic teacher continues to grow in the midst of opposition. The focus also shifts somewhat to highlight his disciples who are to learn from his example.

Chapter fourteen divides into four passages. The first is about John the Baptist (14:1-12), the second the feeding of the five thousand (14:13-21), the third the walking on water (14:22-33), and the fourth a summary passage on Jesus' healing ministry (14:34-36).

The Death of John the Baptist (14:1-12)

[1] At that time Herod the tetrarch heard of the reputation of Jesus [2] and said to his servants, "This man is John the Baptist. He has been raised from the dead; that is why mighty powers are at work in him." [3] Now Herod had arrested John, bound (him), and put him in prison on account of Herodias, the wife of his brother Philip, [4] for John had said to him, "It is not lawful for you to have her." [5] Although he wanted to kill him, he feared the people, for they regarded him as a prophet. [6] But at a birthday celebration for Herod, the daughter of Herodias performed a dance before the guests and delighted Herod [7] so much that he swore to give her whatever she might ask for. [8] Prompted by her mother, she said, "Give me here on a platter the head of John the Baptist." [9] The king was distressed, but because of his oaths and the guests who were present, he ordered that it be given, [10] and he had John beheaded in the prison. [11] His head was brought in on a platter and given to the girl, who took it to her mother. [12] His disciples came and took away the corpse and buried him; and they went and told Jesus.

Jesus' reputation was spreading because of his deeds. The Gospel says that Herod the tetrarch, or Herod Antipas, one of the sons of Herod the Great, had heard of Jesus' "mighty powers" which made him assume that John the Baptist had risen from the dead (14:2). This occasions a remembrance of the beheading of John in a story told out of sequence (14:3-12). The story serves dual purposes. From one angle, it picks up the thread of John the Baptist as an effective prophetic preacher of repentance whose message prepared for that of Jesus (3:1-12). Jesus and John are allied by the content of their message and their prophetic identities. From another angle, the story of John's martyrdom prefigures Jesus' own fate at the hand of another despot, Pontius Pilate. The prophetic ministry in which each is engaged, the fate of which was alluded to at the end of chapter thirteen in the rejection at Nazareth (13:57-58), leads to rejection and martyrdom. From Matthew's perspective, John is in a long line of prophets who have met their demise for the sake of the truth (23:37). Jesus falls in that same category, and he will ask his disciples to do the same. The dramatic story of John's fate injects in the midst of Jesus' compassionate ministry for others a somber note that prophets often meet an ugly end.

Feeding the Five Thousand (14:13-21)

[13] When Jesus heard of it, he withdrew in a boat to a deserted place by himself. The crowds heard of this and followed him on foot from their towns. [14] When he disembarked and saw the vast crowd, his heart was moved with pity for them, and he cured their sick. [15] When it was evening, the disciples approached him and said, "This is a deserted place and it is already late; dismiss the crowds so that they can go to the villages and buy food for themselves." [16] (Jesus) said to them, "There is no need for them to go away; give them some food yourselves." [17] But they said to him, "Five loaves and two fish are all we have here." [18] Then he said, "Bring them here to

me," [19] and he ordered the crowds to sit down on the grass. Taking the five loaves and the two fish, and looking up to heaven, he said the blessing, broke the loaves, and gave them to the disciples, who in turn gave them to the crowds. [20]They all ate and were satisfied, and they picked up the fragments left over—twelve wicker baskets full. [21] Those who ate were about five thousand men, not counting women and children.

Typically, Jesus "withdraws" in the face of such opposition (see 4:12; 12:15; cf. 2:22). Large crowds follow him and at evening they are in a deserted place with no access to food. The disciples want to send them away to get their own food, but Jesus challenges them to give them food. McDonald's or Taco Bell are not an option. Their five loaves and two fish are meager means to serve a hungry mob, but Jesus transforms the situation with eucharistic actions that probably mirror the liturgical life of the Matthean community. The sequence of verbs (looking to heaven → blessing → broke → gave) evokes the eucharistic gestures that still direct the Church's liturgical practice. Jesus' actions provide the miraculous nourishment, but the disciples have their role to play as well. They distribute the meal (v. 19) and later pick up the "fragments" (v. 20, also a liturgical word). That all ate and were satisfied indicates the sufficiency of the miracle. Moreover, it is a deed reminiscent of the prophet Elisha's miraculous feeding in the OT (2 Kgs 4:42-44). Thus, in two short sequences Matthew reinforces Jesus' identity as a prophetic figure whose actions speak of God's special mission. In Jesus, God feeds people and cares for them pastorally.

Walking on Water, and Summary (14:22-36)

[22]Then he made the disciples get into the boat and precede him to the other side, while he dismissed the crowds. [23] After doing so, he went up on the mountain by himself to pray. When it was evening he was there alone. [24] Meanwhile the boat, already a few miles offshore, was being tossed about by the waves, for the wind was against it. [25] During the fourth

watch of the night, he came toward them, walking on the sea. [26] When the disciples saw him walking on the sea they were terrified. "It is a ghost," they said, and they cried out in fear. [27] At once (Jesus) spoke to them, "Take courage, it is I; do not be afraid." [28] Peter said to him in reply, "Lord, if it is you, command me to come to you on the water." [29] He said, "Come." Peter got out of the boat and began to walk on the water toward Jesus. [30] But when he saw how (strong) the wind was he became frightened; and, beginning to sink, he cried out, "Lord, save me!" [31] Immediately Jesus stretched out his hand and caught him, and said to him, "O you of little faith, why did you doubt?" [32] After they got into the boat, the wind died down. [33] Those who were in the boat did him homage, saying, "Truly, you are the Son of God."

On the heels of the feeding of more than five thousand, a different type of miracle occurs when Jesus walks on water in the middle of the night (14:22-33). The disciples are featured in this passage, especially Peter, whose function as their chief spokesman is highlighted. Their primary characteristic is fear, the great enemy of faith. As with the earlier boat scene (8:23-27) the disciples experience fear while in their boat on the water. This time the fear is in seeing Jesus whom they mistake for a ghost (v. 21). Jesus' command to take courage and not be fearful leads Peter to wonder whether it really is Jesus. He offers to come to Jesus over the water at his command. A bold gesture from an overconfident man. When he starts to sink in the waves, all Peter can do is cry out, "Lord save me!" (v. 30; cf. 8:25). His brazen demonstration reveals the cracks in his rock-solid faith. Jesus' reprimand is typical of the disciples in Matthew's Gospel: "O you of little faith, why did you doubt?" (v. 31). Their "little faith," however, is not the same as no faith (cf. 13:58), for they adopt the proper attitude of worship once the wind dies down (v. 33). Matthew portrays the disciples simultaneously as sometimes impetuous and well meaning, bold yet filled with anxiety, and yet finally able to comprehend the mystery that is before them. Peter, in particular, combines these features. As the story proceeds his role as leader among the twelve will expand and be confirmed, but even his faith will not withstand all the trials that can assail it (26:69-75).

> [34]After making the crossing, they came to land at Gennesaret. [35]When the men of that place recognized him, they sent word to all the surrounding country. People brought to him all those who were sick [36]and begged him that they might touch only the tassel on his cloak, and as many as touched it were healed.

The final passage of this chapter provides another summary of Jesus' healing ministry and his reputation (14:34-36; cf. 4:23-25; 9:35-36;14:14). Only touching the tassel of Jesus' cloak is sufficient for healing (v. 36; cf. 9:21). To reach out and touch Jesus is a bold gesture of faith. Faith is not only a matter of assent by words but also by actions. When people seek to touch Jesus and to be touched by him, they place themselves at the disposal of God's healing power.

Jesus and the Scribes and Pharisees (15:1-20)

> [1]Then Pharisees and scribes came to Jesus from Jerusalem and said, [2]"Why do your disciples break the tradition of the elders? They do not wash (their) hands when they eat a meal." [3]He said to them in reply, "And why do you break the commandment of God for the sake of your tradition? [4]For God said, 'Honor your father and your mother,' and 'Whoever curses father or mother shall die.' [5]But you say, 'Whoever says to father or mother, "Any support you might have had from me is dedicated to God," [6]need not honor his father.' You have nullified the word of God for the sake of your tradition. [7]Hypocrites, well did Isaiah prophesy about you when he said:
>
> > [8]'This people honors me with their lips,
> > but their hearts are far from me;

[9] in vain do they worship me,
teaching as doctrines human precepts.' "

[10] He summoned the crowd and said to them, "Hear and understand. [11] It is not what enters one's mouth that defiles that person; but what comes out of the mouth is what defiles one." [12] Then his disciples approached and said to him, "Do you know that the Pharisees took offense when they heard what you said?" [13] He said in reply, "Every plant that my heavenly Father has not planted will be uprooted. [14] Let them alone; they are blind guides [of the blind]. If a blind person leads a blind person, both will fall into a pit." [15] Then Peter said to him in reply, "Explain [this] parable to us." [16] He said to them, "Are even you still without understanding? [17] Do you not realize that everything that enters the mouth passes into the stomach and is expelled into the latrine? [18] But the things that come out of the mouth come from the heart, and they defile. [19] For from the heart come evil thoughts, murder, adultery, unchastity, theft, false witness, blasphemy. [20] These are what defile a person, but to eat with unwashed hands does not defile."

This passage that opens chapter fifteen shifts the focus somewhat with a dispute between Jesus and some scribes and Pharisees from Jerusalem (15:1-20). This lengthy discussion starts with a practical question: "Why do your disciples break the tradition of the elders?" (v. 2). The example they give is the failure to wash their hands before eating. This is not a mere matter of hygiene. It was part of a series of sacred rituals to maintain purity in the eyes of God. Jesus' response indicates the more profound failure of his opponents. In worrying about the adherence to such traditions tied to strict religious beliefs, they fail to live up to the weightier matters of the Law and thus show themselves as hypocrites (vv. 3-9). They uphold mere human traditions while violating God's commands. Jesus again relies on the prophetic word of Isaiah the prophet (Is 29:13) to explain that they only pay lip service to God's Law (vv. 8-9). He then informs the crowd of the essential nature of conforming the interior with the exterior. One's beliefs should be reflected in one's actions and vice versa (vv. 10-20). A cursory glance at this passage might mislead us to think the debate was merely over matters of Jewish religious practice. This is not the case, for every religion can potentially fall into the trap of placing less important regulations or traditions ahead of the essentials. Jesus' reminder that so many human evils come from the heart should make us circumspect (v. 19). Matthew really is a moralist, but he tries to get us to see the "big picture" so that we might do better in the little things of life.

The Faith of the Canaanite Woman (15:21-28)

[21] Then Jesus went from that place and withdrew to the region of Tyre and Sidon. [22] And behold, a Canaanite woman of that district came and called out, "Have pity on me, Lord, Son of David! My daughter is tormented by a demon." [23] But he did not say a word in answer to her. His disciples came and asked him, "Send her away, for she keeps calling out after us." [24] He said in reply, "I was sent only to the lost sheep of the house of Israel." [25] But the woman came and did him homage, saying, "Lord, help me." [26] He said in reply, "It is not right to take the food of the children and throw it to the dogs." [27] She said, "Please, Lord, for even the dogs eat the scraps that fall from the table of their masters." [28] Then Jesus said to her in reply, "O woman, great is your faith! Let it be done for you as you wish." And her daughter was healed from that hour.

Three more miracle stories round out chapter fifteen. After the controversy, Jesus goes to the area around Tyre and Sidon, Gentile territory (cf. 11:22). A Gentile woman cries out to Jesus for help for her daughter who is possessed by a demon. Despite her plea, Jesus maintains that he is oriented only to the house of Israel (v. 24). Her persistence, however, takes over. She pleads for assistance, to which Jesus responds with a curiously unsympathetic view of not wasting children's food on dogs, as if to say as a Gentile she is not worthy to receive what is meant for the

Jews. (Jews sometimes likened Gentiles to "dogs.") Her quick comeback turns the tables, for she mentions that even dogs get the scraps from their master's table (v. 27). Her response is not disrespectful. She still addresses Jesus as "Lord," and Jesus immediately commends her faith and grants the miracle. Her tactful persistence wins over Jesus' compassion even though she is an outsider, not one of the lost sheep of the house of Israel (10:5-6; 15:24). God's mercy really is wide and God's grace flows in all directions, but we must also be willing to put our needs boldly before the Lord.

Another summary passage follows that describes Jesus' miracles and their effects (15:29-31). The setting is important in this instance, for just as Jesus ascended the mountain to sit and teach his first sermon (5:1), so he ascends a mountain here to sit and perform miracles (v. 29). The mountain is both a place of revelation of God's will and a place to witness God's saving power. The final miracle, the feeding of the four thousand (15:32-39), takes place in the same setting. Reminiscent of Isaiah's vision of Mount Zion as a setting for God's final banquet, Jesus' actions prefigure the eschatological feast (Is 25:6-9). It repeats essentially the same story as the feeding of the five thousand but with some nuance. The disciples do not try to dismiss the crowds this time but only wonder how they can be fed. This is a small measure of growth in their understanding. They have only seven loaves and a few fish, but the same basic eucharistic action takes place (gave thanks → broke → gave). Jesus effects the miracle and his disciples distribute the results and pick up the leftovers. Once more Jesus demonstrates his compassion and ability to nourish people not only in word but in action. I might add that the curious line of "not counting women and children" (v. 38; cf. 14:21) is not meant as an insult. First, it reflects historically that, in Jesus' day, women and children were secondary citizens. It also helps to heighten the effect of the two miraculous feedings. Jesus feeds, respectively, 5000 and 4000 men, let alone the women and children.

All are fed, and the numbers are phenomenal, given the lack of resources. Jesus' power knows no bounds.

The final segment of this part of the Gospel consists of a further controversy and the confession by Peter of Jesus' identity (16:1-20). Jesus' opponents, named as the Pharisees and Sadducees whom Matthew understands to be allied against Jesus, still seek signs, some concrete evidence that he represents a higher authority (v. 1). Jesus responds that they have the ability to use folk knowledge to read the portents of the sky in order to predict the weather, but they fail to read the more essential signs of God's kingdom. Jesus repeats the message he had stated earlier: An evil generation seeks signs, but the only sign will be that of repentance (v. 4; cf. 12:39). This brief exchange leads to a warning Jesus gives to his disciples by means of a metaphor (16:5-12). Jesus cautions them about the "leaven" of the Pharisees and the Sadducees, meaning their teaching (v. 12). These words specifically conjure up the prior two miraculous feedings of people that the disciples had witnessed but failed to comprehend. They think that Jesus warns that they have no bread along with them (vv. 7-8). Their "little faith" and lack of full comprehension comes to the fore again. Despite their attention and their desire, and even their participation in the feedings, they do not see that Jesus has the ability to provide for whatever they need if only they would have more faith. Ancient peoples considered leaven a sinister and mysterious element because it magically made bread rise. It makes a perfect image for sinister "teaching" that goes contrary to the aims of the gospel message. Even after two miraculous feedings, the disciples need to grow in faith. It is not something that can remain stagnant.

The Confession of Peter (16:13-20)

13 When Jesus went into the region of Caesarea Philippi he asked his disciples, "Who do people say that the Son of Man is?" 14 They replied, "Some say John the Baptist, others Elijah,

115

still others Jeremiah or one of the prophets." [15] He said to them, "But who do you say that I am?" [16] Simon Peter said in reply, "You are the Messiah, the Son of the living God." [17] Jesus said to him in reply, "Blessed are you, Simon son of Jonah. For flesh and blood has not revealed this to you, but my heavenly Father. [18] And so I say to you, you are Peter, and upon this rock I will build my church, and the gates of the netherworld shall not prevail against it. [19] I will give you the keys to the kingdom of heaven. Whatever you bind on earth shall be bound in heaven; and whatever you loose on earth shall be loosed in heaven." [20] Then he strictly ordered his disciples to tell no one that he was the Messiah.

The final scene in this section is the well-known confession of Peter at Caesarea Philippi, in the northern part of Galilee (16:13-20). This time Jesus is the one who poses the question of his identity. It brings the understandable response that some people think of him as John the Baptist (remember Herod, 14:2), or a prophet such as Elijah (forerunner of the messiah) or Jeremiah (the suffering prophet, par excellence). Jesus retorts with the more crucial question, "But who do you say that I am?" (v. 15). This question reaches out from the pages of the Gospel and confronts disciples of every generation. Our understanding of Jesus' identity, and thereby his significance, is central to the faith. Throughout his story of Jesus, Matthew has focused in obvious and subtle ways on this question. On it hinges the estimate of how little or how great our faith has become.

Peter's response, that Jesus is the messiah, the Son of God, is absolutely correct from a christological perspective. Jesus endorses it swiftly and confirms that it is a divine revelation not just human perception (v. 17, "flesh and blood"). Then something extraordinary takes place that only occurs in Matthew. Jesus commends Simon Peter as "blessed" and bestows on him an authority that rivals that of the Jewish religious leaders, the ability to "bind and loose." Moreover, Jesus gives Peter the "keys to the kingdom of heaven" and asserts that Peter is a "rock" on which the Church is to be built (vv. 18-19). He whose faith has thus far been rather shaky, is now to be the firm foundation of the new community of faith called "Church," the assembly of faithful ones gathered in the name of the Lord Jesus. Binding and loosing refers to the authority to makes rules and pass judgments that God will ratify. There can be no doubt that Peter is given a prominent position of authority within Matthew's community. He who serves as spokesman for the other disciples also has a distinct role in the authority structure of the new community. Most encouraging is that fact that Matthew does not hide Peter's failures in other ways. He denied Jesus and his faith at times wavered, but these did not prevent him from becoming the rock of faith that could withstand even the assaults of the devil (v. 18).

Catholics see in this image the special Petrine ministry of the pope to promote unity and to provide authoritative leadership. Even non-Catholics have acknowledged that Peter had a special and prominent role in the early Christian community. Although contemporary denominations differ on how to interpret the power and authority of Peter's successors, Matthew gives a clear image of how he viewed the matter. The Church needed leadership when Jesus left his earthly ministry in the care of his disciples. Their world-wide ministry of evangelization would require discipline and direction. Peter, above all, provided these and gives the rallying point for the Church's ministry. This time-honored tradition, however, needs to be balanced by the next passage of the Gospel which focuses on the limits of Peter's understanding of Jesus' identity. This confession climaxes this part of the Gospel and leads to a major shift in the story. If Peter is given important power and authority in the Church, it is not so that he can lord it over others and exalt his position. He must reckon also with the real goal of ministry which Jesus will expound in the rest of the Gospel.

V

The Ministry of Jesus
and the Cost of Discipleship
(16:21–25:46)

Discipleship and the Cross (16:21-28)

[21] From that time on, Jesus began to show his disciples that he must go to Jerusalem and suffer greatly from the elders, the chief priests, and the scribes, and be killed and on the third day be raised. [22] Then Peter took him aside and began to rebuke him, "God forbid, Lord! No such thing shall ever happen to you." [23] He turned and said to Peter, "Get behind me, Satan! You are an obstacle to me. You are thinking not as God does, but as human beings do."

[24] Then Jesus said to his disciples, "Whoever wishes to come after me must deny himself, take up his cross, and follow me. [25] For whoever wishes to save his life will lose it, but whoever loses his life for my sake will find it. [26] What profit would there be for one to gain the whole world and forfeit his life? Or what can one give in exchange for his life? [27] For the Son of Man will come with his angels in his Father's glory, and then he will repay everyone according to his conduct. [28] Amen, I say to you, there are some standing here who will not taste death until they see the Son of Man coming in his kingdom."

After Peter's confession another major turning point in the Gospel occurs with the expression, "From that time on, Jesus began to *show* his disciples . . ." (16:21; cf. 4:17). The content of this verse is the first of three main passion/resurrection predictions (cf. 17:22-23; 20:17-19). Jesus not only preaches and teaches but now he will begin to "show" his disciples what he is truly about. The emphasis from this point forward is on Jesus' coming sacrifice and the need for the disciples to learn more profoundly what it means to follow him. Whereas he had pronounced Jesus' identity correctly in the previous passage (16:13-19), here Peter shows himself once more to be obtuse. His response to Jesus' teaching about the necessity of his passion and death at the hands of his enemies is one of disbelief. Peter privately rebukes Jesus, to which Jesus speaks the harshest words of retribution directed against Peter. He calls him "Satan" and a stumbling block (NAB "obstacle"; Greek *skandalon*, v. 23; cf. 13:41; 18:7). He unwittingly becomes an instrument for others' failure to perceive Jesus' ministry properly. He causes others to stumble in their faith. Peter's lack of acceptance of Jesus' fate indicates that he is still caught in the limitations of human perception. He has not progressed to God's perspective.

These two passages about Peter that bridge two distinct sections of the Gospel must be held in tandem. Peter's accurate confession of Jesus' identity is coupled with his unwillingness to accept what that identity means. To confess him as Son of God seems easy compared to understanding him as Son of Man who will offer his life for all humanity. Jesus came not for himself but to suffer for the sake of others. Peter, too, has his strengths and limitations. He is commended for his partial but accurate insight but sternly reprimanded for his inability to move to the deeper understanding of Jesus' messianic identity. Position does not necessarily preserve one from misperception of God's will.

In the wake of this exchange Jesus once more addresses his disciples about the true nature of their call (16:24-28). It entails:

- self-denial

- taking up one's cross and following Jesus

- losing one's life for Jesus' sake in order to preserve it eternally

- standing vigilant until the Son of Man comes in his glory for judgment.

The teaching concludes with a prediction that God's judgment will arrive very soon, in fact, before some of those hearing Jesus' words would die (v. 28). Obviously this did not occur exactly as predicted, but we should not worry over it. Jesus and his disciples expected an imminent end to the world as we know it. It was a natural part of their world under the influence of apocalyptic thought that developed in Judaism. Christians in various ages, including our own at the end of the second millennium, have expected God's kingdom soon. We should not become preoccupied with seeking a timetable (see Mk 13:32; 1 Thes 5:1-2). That is also not Matthew's main point here. The focus is rather on the sacrifices required of true disciples.

The Transfiguration of Jesus (17:1-13)

Chapter seventeen continues the teaching about discipleship from a different perspective and in the context of Jesus' identity. The chapter divides into five parts: the transfiguration of Jesus (17:1-8), the teaching about Elijah (17:9-13), a healing (17:14-20), the second passion prediction (17:22-23), and a mysterious controversy over taxation (17:24-27).

[1] After six days Jesus took Peter, James, and John his brother, and led them up a high mountain by themselves. [2] And he was transfigured before them; his face shone like the sun and his clothes became white as light. [3] And behold, Moses and Elijah appeared to them, conversing with him. [4] Then Peter said to Jesus in reply, "Lord, it is good that we are here. If you wish, I will make three tents here, one for you, one for Moses, and one for Elijah." [5] While he was still speaking, behold, a bright cloud cast a shadow over them, then

from the cloud came a voice that said, "This is my beloved Son, with whom I am well pleased; listen to him." ⁶When the disciples heard this, they fell prostrate and were very much afraid. ⁷But Jesus came and touched them, saying, "Rise, and do not be afraid." ⁸And when the disciples raised their eyes, they saw no one else but Jesus alone.

⁹ As they were coming down from the mountain, Jesus charged them, "Do not tell the vision to anyone until the Son of Man has been raised from the dead."

The transfiguration story involves the inner circle of Jesus' disciples, Peter, James and John, whom Jesus takes up a high mountain. They who were first called (4:18-22) now are privileged to glimpse the glory that will come with Jesus' embrace of his true identity as God's Son. While they are on the mountain, the special place of revelation, Jesus becomes bright like the sun and Moses and Elijah appear conversing with him. These two figures represent the best of the "old," the Law and the prophets. Impetuous Peter immediately desires to pitch a tent and stay awhile, but instead a voice comes from the clouds that harks back to Jesus' baptism: "This is my beloved Son, with whom I am well pleased; listen to him" (17:5; cf. 3:17). OT imagery permeates the entire scene, yet something new occurs. Jesus' identity is once more confirmed, but his disciples are instructed more clearly to listen to his teaching. They have gotten glimpses of God's kingdom before (the parables) and have partially caught onto the gospel message. Now they glimpse the glory that will come from the sacrifice of Jesus, but they are also instructed to pay more attention. Unfortunately, we all probably have a bit of Peter in us. We get part of the message, but not the whole thing. When we do have those precious moments of insight and revelation, we might also be tempted to stay put, to dwell on the mountain where we can always be present to the glory that is God. But life is not lived on the mountain. It is lived in the valleys and plains of everyday activity. Jesus reassures his disciples that there is nothing to fear

(v. 7), but they also must descend from the mountain (v. 9). In the Church's liturgy the transfiguration story appears on the second Sunday in Lent. It is a reminder in the midst of Lenten penance and sacrifice that the necessity of suffering is not in vain but leads to a glory that will arrive one day.

> [10] Then the disciples asked him, "Why do the scribes say that Elijah must come first?" [11] He said in reply, "Elijah will indeed come and restore all things; [12] but I tell you that Elijah has already come, and they did not recognize him but did to him whatever they pleased. So also will the Son of Man suffer at their hands." [13] Then the disciples understood that he was speaking to them of John the Baptist.

The transfiguration gives way to a discussion about Elijah (17:10-13). The disciples note that Elijah is to come before the messiah, and Jesus acknowledges this but attaches an important addendum, namely, that Elijah had already come in the person of John the Baptist (cf. 11:7-14). This statement confirms essentially that the messianic days have arrived in Jesus. Just as Israel rejected John and had him put to death, so will this happen to the "Son of Man," the christological title most associated with the passion and death of Jesus (17:12; cf. 17:23; 20:18).

Healing of the Possessed Boy and a Second Prophecy of the Passion (17:14-23)

> [14] When they came to the crowd a man approached, knelt down before him, [15] and said, "Lord, have pity on my son, for he is a lunatic and suffers severely; often he falls into fire, and often into water. [16] I brought him to your disciples, but they could not cure him." [17] Jesus said in reply, "O faithless and perverse generation, how long will I be with you? How long will I endure you? Bring him here to me." [18] Jesus rebuked him and the demon came out of him, and from that hour the boy was cured. [19] Then the disciples approached Jesus in private

and said, "Why could we not drive it out?" [20]He said to them, "Because of your little faith. Amen, I say to you, if you have faith the size of a mustard seed, you will say to this mountain, 'Move from here to there,' and it will move. Nothing will be impossible for you."

The healing of the boy possessed by a demon takes place next (17:14-20; v. 21 is omitted in most manuscripts and probably comes from Mark). The boy's father approaches Jesus reverently by kneeling and addressing him as "Lord," making his request known. An added detail is that Jesus' disciples had tried to heal the boy unsuccessfully. The point of this miracle is not merely christological, to show Jesus' power, but also ecclesiological, to emphasize once more the necessity of firm faith on the part of the disciples. Jesus explains that their attempt did not work because of their "little faith" (v. 20; cf. 6:30; 8:26; 14:31; 16:8). Paradoxically, although their faith is contrasted to the "faithless and perverse generation" around them (v. 17), Jesus instructs the disciples that if they had the faith of a tiny mustard seed, they would be able to move mountains (v. 20). Just how little is *their* faith? Just how little faith can be effective? Faith, for Matthew, is not assent to a series of beliefs but a relationship with God and with Jesus. It is a quality of trust and absolute confidence. Fear and doubt interfere with faith, but they do not defeat it. Matthew's presentation of this miracle story squarely confronts the faith of the disciples and provides ongoing encouragement to keep striving for that quality of faith that will allow us to accomplish anything (v. 20).

> [22] As they were gathering in Galilee, Jesus said to them, "The Son of Man is to be handed over to men, [23]and they will kill him, and he will be raised on the third day." And they were overwhelmed with grief.

Then Jesus interjects a reminder that discipleship is not easy. He pronounces the second passion prediction, to which the disciples respond with grief (17:22-23). Matthew does not conceive of suffering as something simple but profound. We would be unrealistic if we embraced it naively thinking that it will not cause us great grief.

The Temple Tax (17:24-27)

[24] When they came to Capernaum, the collectors of the temple tax approached Peter and said, "Doesn't your teacher pay the temple tax?" [25] "Yes," he said. When he came into the house, before he had time to speak, Jesus asked him, "What is your opinion, Simon? From whom do the kings of the earth take tolls or census tax? From their subjects or from foreigners?" [26] When he said, "From foreigners," Jesus said to him, "Then the subjects are exempt. [27] But that we may not offend them, go to the sea, drop in a hook, and take the first fish that comes up. Open its mouth and you will find a coin worth twice the temple tax. Give that to them for me and for you."

The chapter concludes with a story about taxes set in Capernaum (17:24-27). People have probably always dreaded taxes. In biblical times, however, taxes could be crushing. At issue is the Temple tax paid by Jews for the upkeep of the Temple in Jerusalem. This curious story might seem to have a secular message except that we should remember Matthew's Jewishness. Paying the Temple tax was a serious religious obligation. In the evangelist's time the Temple was already destroyed, but the story likely originated earlier when it was still standing. The religious principle involved is not giving scandal (v. 27, NAB "not offend"). The coin miraculously found in the fish's mouth serves for both Jesus' and Peter's obligatory tax. There is also a subtle christological message hidden in the story. Jesus, as God's Son, had no obligation to pay the Temple tax, for the Temple was his Father's house (21:13). Despite his unique position, Jesus opts not to give scandal. The general principle is a good one. Sometimes, even though we are not obligated by certain religious constraints, conformity to a specific regulation avoids the possibility of scandalizing someone. In Matthew's case, this story provides another avenue to honor the Jewish origins of his community even while acknowledging the new community that has emerged.

Becoming Like a Child (18:1-10)

[1] At that time the disciples approached Jesus and said, "Who is the greatest in the kingdom of heaven?" [2] He called a child over, placed it in their midst, [3] and said, "Amen, I say to you, unless you turn and become like children, you will not enter the kingdom of heaven. [4] Whoever humbles himself like this child is the greatest in the kingdom of heaven.

[5] "And whoever receives one child such as this in my name receives me. [6] Whoever causes one of these little ones who believe in me to sin, it would be better for him to have a great millstone hung around his neck and to be drowned in the depths of the sea. [7] Woe to the world because of things that cause sin! Such things must come, but woe to the one through whom they come! [8] If your hand or foot causes you to sin, cut it off and throw it away. It is better for you to enter into life maimed or crippled than with two hands or two feet to be thrown into eternal fire. [9] And if your eye causes you to sin, tear it out and throw it away. It is better for you to enter into life with one eye than with two eyes to be thrown into fiery Gehenna. [10] See that you do not despise one of these little ones, for I say to you that their angels in heaven always look upon the face of my heavenly Father."

Chapter eighteen continues Jesus' instructions by means of a fourth discourse. It centers on the theme of discipleship, concluding with a verse from chapter nineteen that repeats the formula seen at the end of major discourses (18:1–19:1). This discourse of Matthew's Gospel is sometimes labeled the "community discourse." Its primary focus is on behavior in the midst of the community of disciples, the Church, even though it may be directed to the leaders of the community as much as to the community itself.

The chapter is set into motion by the disciples' question about who is greatest in the kingdom. The question itself indicates a lack of understanding about what Jesus has been teaching all along. People are obsessed with position and power. Being famous and having the places of honor are important. Psychologists indicate that people with bad self images will go to great lengths for recognition and status, even to the point of notoriety. Almost everyone wants to be recognized as somebody important. Jesus' response to the query, however, is quite concrete. He stands a child in their midst and says that becoming like a child is essential to entering the kingdom of God (18:1-5). In essence, the image directs the rest of the discourse, because at every step along the way the values of discipleship that go counter to the norm in ordinary society take precedence. Discipleship does not mean being tall but small. Like the earlier discourse to the disciples (ch. 10), I will summarize this chapter's content with a checklist of the values of discipleship.

According to Jesus, discipleship in the new community of the Church involves the following:

- humility like that of children ("little ones") who have little status in society (vv. 4-5,6,10,14)

- resisting temptation steadfastly (vv. 6-9)

- repenting for one's sinfulness like a lost sheep that is found (vv. 10-14)

- reconciling directly with those who cause trouble in the community (vv. 15-18)

- praying together for the good of the community (v. 19)

- forgiving one another from the heart (vv. 21-35).

126

The message is straightforward enough. The values are consistent both with those enunciated in the Sermon on the Mount (ch. 5–7) and in the disciples' discourse (ch. 10). Yet there are nuances and novelties in the midst of these ethical instructions. Throughout the discourse the repeated phrase "little ones" emphasizes the lowly stature the disciples are to assume vis-à-vis the world. Also, the hyperbolic language used in connection with the instruction on temptations (vv. 6-9) and the two parables of the lost sheep (vv. 10-14) and the unforgiving servant (vv. 21-35) are typical of the extravagance of God's kingdom (ch. 13). The kingdom's values require a formidable commitment, but one does not need to be excessively literal in the advice about cutting off a hand or foot or plucking out an eye that causes one to sin (vv. 8-9).

Parable of the Lost Sheep (18:10-14)

[10] "See that you do not despise one of these little ones, for I say to you that their angels in heaven always look upon the face of my heavenly Father. [11] [12] What is your opinion? If a man has a hundred sheep and one of them goes astray, will he not leave the ninety-nine in the hills and go in search of the stray? [13] And if he finds it, amen, I say to you, he rejoices more over it than over the ninety-nine that did not stray. [14] In just the same way, it is not the will of your heavenly Father that one of these little ones be lost."

The parable of the lost sheep itself is bidirectional in its message (vv. 10-14; verse 11 is omitted because it is likely an addition from Luke 19:10). On the one hand, it promotes an image of security that even one "lost sheep" is of value to the community. On the other hand, it challenges the community and its leaders actively to seek out those who go astray because God does not will one of the "little ones" to be lost (v. 14). Any community knows that some members stray or wander off, but more may be meant here. The verb "goes astray" (NAB) is actually in the passive voice, meaning "to be led astray" (*planethe*). Some in Matthew's own community may have been led astray by others, that is, corrupted in their discipleship. They became apostates. They did not necessarily give up their faith on their own but were seduced away from it (cf. 13:22). All the more reason to seek them out. Bringing back the lost sheep was an essential part of Jesus' mission (9:36; 12:11; 15:24) and a fulfillment of God's own promise (Ez 34:11-12). I must admit that this issue is a delicate one. There are times when leaders, in particular, are happy to see the troublemakers in the community go elsewhere. Those who rock the boat are often too much bother. Jesus asks us to resist the temptation to allow this to happen. He has come to seek the lost. The community of disciples is also to reach out and actively seek those who leave. This may go contrary to our tendencies, but it is the nature of God to do just that.

The Life of Community (18:15-35)

[15] "If your brother sins [against you], go and tell him his fault between you and him alone. If he listens to you, you have won over your brother. [16] If he does not listen, take one or two others along with you, so that 'every fact may be established on the testimony of two or three witnesses.' [17] If he refuses to listen to them, tell the Church. If he refuses to listen even to the Church, then treat him as you would a Gentile or a tax collector. [18] Amen, I say to you, whatever you bind on earth shall be bound in heaven, and whatever you loose on earth shall be loosed in heaven."

Another noteworthy teaching concerns a more specific way for the community to treat those who cause trouble in it (18:15-18). It sets out what ought to be a standard three-step process in all communities, whether Christian or not:

1) confront the offender directly and privately to seek a change of heart (v. 15)

128

2) if that fails, bring along two or three others to assist in resolving the matter (v. 16)
3) if that, too, fails, then "tell the Church" and treat that person like a Gentile or tax collector (v. 17).

No passage in Matthew is as down-to-earth and practical as this one, yet it is one of the most difficult to put into practice. The first step to correct the fault of another is a direct encounter with the offender. If that is not effective, one can get assistance. Matthew probably alludes to the Jewish tradition of two or three being necessary as witnesses (Dt 19:15). Only as a last resort does one go to a higher authority.

Many times I have witnessed a passive-aggressive way of treating problems in the Christian community. Few people like direct confrontation. Maybe fewer yet are good at "tough love," confronting someone lovingly yet firmly in order to correct destructive behavior. Sadly, I think the tendency of most people is to run to a higher authority figure to have someone's fault confronted or corrected. Interestingly, in connection with this procedure, the community (or its collective leadership) is given the same authority as Peter with reference to binding and loosing (v. 18; cf. 16:19). The community has the same responsibility and privilege of regulating ethical behavior as does its primary leader. These are not to be seen as competitive authorities but complementary.

Treating a recalcitrant member as a Gentile or tax collector may at first seem like making them outcasts, but we should remember that Jesus called such to be members of his inner circle and his wider community (9:9-10; 10:3; 11:19; 21:31). In other words, they become new "targets" for evangelization and being brought back to the fold, thus connecting the procedure with the preceding image of the lost sheep.

[19]"Again, [amen,] I say to you, if two of you agree on earth about anything for which they are to pray, it shall be granted to them by my heavenly Father. [20]For where two or three are

gathered together in my name, there am I in the midst of them."

A final directive rounds out this advice. Jesus urges the community to pray together, "[f]or wherever two or three are gathered together in my name, there am I in the midst of them" (v. 20). Jesus' abiding presence in the community is the surest sign that he is "with us" (1:23; 28:20), no matter how large or small that community might be. In comparison to Judaism that required a minimum of ten men to constitute a community of prayer, Jesus' attitude of expecting only two or three reflects a new liberalism. This line of the Gospel may be its most often quoted. It always reminds us that our expectations about the faith need not be extravagant, even if God's own graciousness is. Numbers don't measure success; quality of faith does.

Forgiveness (18:21-35)

[21] Then Peter approaching asked him, "Lord, if my brother sins against me, how often must I forgive him? As many as seven times?" [22] Jesus answered, "I say to you, not seven times but seventy-seven times. [23] That is why the kingdom of heaven may be likened to a king who decided to settle accounts with his servants. [24] When he began the accounting, a debtor was brought before him who owed him a huge amount. [25] Since he had no way of paying it back, his master ordered him to be sold, along with his wife, his children, and all his property, in payment of the debt. [26] At that, the servant fell down, did him homage, and said, 'Be patient with me, and I will pay you back in full.' [27] Moved with compassion the master of that servant let him go and forgave him the loan. [28] When that servant had left, he found one of his fellow servants who owed him a much smaller amount. He seized him and started to choke him, demanding, 'Pay back what you owe.' [29] Falling to his knees, his fellow servant begged him, 'Be patient with me, and I will pay you back.' [30] But he refused. Instead, he had him put in prison until he paid back the debt.

³¹Now when his fellow servants saw what had happened, they were deeply disturbed, and went to their master and reported the whole affair. ³² His master summoned him and said to him, 'You wicked servant! I forgave you your entire debt because you begged me to. ³³ Should you not have had pity on your fellow servant, as I had pity on you?' ³⁴Then in anger his master handed him over to the torturers until he should pay back the whole debt. ³⁵ So will my heavenly Father do to you, unless each of you forgives his brother from his heart."

The final passage in the chapter is a lengthy parable about an unforgiving servant given in response to another query by Peter about how many times one should forgive an offender (18:21-35). This story flows nicely from the previous two which also focused on wandering or problematic members of the community. Just how tolerant must we be of deviance in the community's standards? One gets the impression that Matthew's community was no bed of roses. Internal troubles were rife and they needed advice about how to deal with them. Here is where Jesus' most penetrating teaching on forgiveness and reconciliation takes on mammoth significance. To forgive seven times, the perfect biblical number, would be considered excessively patient. To do so seventy times seven times, implying an inconceivable infinity, is hopelessly extravagant. Sometimes one's offer of forgiveness, however, bears no fruit in the way we apply it to others. Jesus' teaching in this parable is that the forgiveness shown to us by God is something we should also show to one another, in fulfillment of the way we have been taught to pray in the Lord's Prayer (6:12). History, including Christian history, provides endless examples of harboring grudges that bring people to eternal acts of vengeance upon vengeance. Some regions of the world exhibit centuries of senseless and cyclic revenge. Consider Ireland, the Holy Land, and the Balkan states. The inability to forgive often leads to endless reprisals. Religion, in fact, has been the cause of incredible wars and atrocities over the ages, and Christianity has not been exempted from these tendencies. But Jesus' teaching on forgiveness stands at the very core of what God's kingdom entails. The parable of the unforgiving servant illustrates this stance. Forgiveness from the heart is not an option for disciples of Jesus but a requirement.

With this discourse concluded, Jesus leaves Galilee and goes to Judea and Jerusalem where he will embrace his fate (19:1). From chapter nineteen onward, Matthew more closely follows Mark's story of Jesus and there is much that overlaps. Matthew never loses his distinctiveness, however. The next two chapters lead to the triumphal entry into Jerusalem and provide further ethical teaching and instruction on discipleship (ch. 19–20). Matthew does not tire of showing us Jesus as an effective teacher and healer, all the while modeling for his disciples that they will have to confront the same fate that awaits him.

Marriage, Divorce and Celibacy (19:3-12)

³ Some Pharisees approached him, and tested him, saying, "Is it lawful for a man to divorce his wife for any cause whatever?" ⁴ He said in reply, "Have you not read that from the beginning the Creator 'made them male and female' ⁵ and said, 'For this reason a man shall leave his father and mother and be joined to his wife, and the two shall become one flesh'? ⁶ So they are no longer two, but one flesh. Therefore, what God has joined together, no human being must separate." ⁷ They said to him, "Then why did Moses command that the man give the woman a bill of divorce and dismiss [her]?" ⁸ He said to them, "Because of the hardness of your hearts Moses allowed you to divorce your wives, but from the beginning it was not so. ⁹ I say to you, whoever divorces his wife [unless the marriage is unlawful] and marries another commits adultery." ¹⁰ [His] disciples said to him, "If that is the case of a man with his wife, it is better not to marry." ¹¹ He answered, "Not all can accept [this] word, but only those to whom that is granted. ¹² Some are incapable of marriage because they

were born so; some, because they were made so by others; some, because they have renounced marriage for the sake of the kingdom of heaven. Whoever can accept this ought to accept it."

The first verse of chapter 19 is the standard Matthean formula that concludes the previous discourse and provides a transition to the events and teachings of chapters 19–20 ("When Jesus finished these words . . ."). The topics vary but reinforce and expand what Jesus has already taught. The first topic Jesus addresses is the thorny problem of divorce (19:3-12). The Pharisees provide the question to "test" Jesus. Their intention betrays their allegiance to the forces of evil that try to trap Jesus and ultimately destroy him (v. 3 *peirazo;* cf. 4:1,3; 16:1; 22:18,35). Jesus turns the tables on them by addressing their question, in very Jewish fashion, with the biblical tradition from Genesis that clearly shows the ideal of marriage between a woman and a man as rooted in the sacred order of creation (Gn 1:27; 2:21-24). The teaching here is no different from what Jesus had given in the Sermon on the Mount (5:31-32), but it is expanded considerably and placed in a narrative rather than legal setting. Jesus' teaching can be outlined in three stages. First, he reminds his opponents of the ideal of marriage created by God (vv. 4-6). God intended that a man and a woman would be joined and become "one flesh"; this is the sacred mystery of marriage that explains both sexual attraction and the deep human need to be loved. Second, Jesus does not gloss over the fact that Jewish law permitted men to divorce their wives in some circumstances (vv. 7-9; cf. Dt 24:1-4). According to Jesus, however, the reason was the stubbornness of the Israelites and not because God intended it so. Finally, the disciples respond to Jesus' repetition of the ideal of marriage with a sarcastic comment that it might be better to remain single (v. 10), to which Jesus explains that not marrying is a difficult challenge that applies to some but not to all (vv. 11-12).

This lengthier teaching on marriage, divorce and celibacy includes the exception clause we saw earlier in the Sermon on the Mount which is difficult to translate with precision (cf. 5:32; 19:9; *porneia*). There is at least one instance (unlawful marriage? adultery?) which the Matthean community recognized as permitting legitimate divorce, but the general rule remains the same: divorce and remarriage are alien to the gospel message. This teaching remains even more challenging today in our "throwaway" society. It is easier to run away, to change one's situation, or not to bother at all with a marriage commitment, than it is to work hard at establishing a loving, faithful, monogamous relationship. In fact, we live in a society that seems genuinely frightened of any permanent commitments. We prefer to leave our options open. Jesus reminds his opponents and his disciples that taking the easy path out of a difficult situation runs counter to God's intention. Like a stern athletic coach, Jesus keeps the expectations—the goal—high. He urges his followers to knuckle down and work hard. Our modern tendency to trivialize or sentimentalize love has no place in Jesus' vision. We cannot escape the reality that authentic, enduring human love is difficult to achieve and maintain in the ideal, but that must never prevent us from striving after it.

Jesus and the Little Children (19:13-15)

¹³ Then children were brought to him that he might lay his hands on them and pray. The disciples rebuked them, ¹⁴ but Jesus said, "Let the children come to me, and do not prevent them; for the kingdom of heaven belongs to such as these." ¹⁵ After he placed his hands on them, he went away.

There follows a brief passage describing Jesus' response to the presence of children (19:13-15). The stated purpose is so that Jesus "might lay his hands on them and pray," but the disciples rebuke them (v. 13). Ironically, the disciples try to prevent the presence of these "little ones" whom Jesus presents to them as ideals of discipleship (cf. 18:3). In the context of Judaism, which did not permit the participation of children (except, at times, only male children) in religious formalities, Jesus' welcome of children is another startling ideal. They belong to the "kingdom" as much or even more than those who think *they* do. This brief teaching coincides with the previous ideal of marriage and also prepares for the more difficult teaching that follows. The kingdom of God offers a very different vision than what we imagine (19:12,14,24).

The Rich Young Man (19:16-30)

[16]Now someone approached him and said, "Teacher, what good must I do to gain eternal life?" [17] He answered him, "Why do you ask me about the good? There is only One who is good. If you wish to enter into life, keep the commandments." [18] He asked him, "Which ones?" And Jesus replied, "'You shall not kill; you shall not commit adultery; you shall not steal; you shall not bear false witness; [19]honor your father and your mother'; and 'you shall love your neighbor as yourself.'" [20] The young man said to him, "All of these I have observed. What do I still lack?" [21] Jesus said to him, "If you wish to be perfect, go, sell what you have and give to [the] poor, and you will have treasure in heaven. Then come, follow me." [22]When the young man heard this statement, he went away sad, for he had many possessions. [23] Then Jesus said to his disciples, "Amen, I say to you, it will be hard for one who is rich to enter the kingdom of heaven. [24]Again I say to you, it is easier for a camel to pass through the eye of a needle than for one who is rich to enter the kingdom of God." [25]When the disciples heard this, they were greatly astonished and said, "Who then can be saved?" [26] Jesus looked at them and said, "For human beings this is impossible, but for God all things are possible." [27] Then Peter said to him in reply, "We have given up everything and followed you. What will there be for us?" [28]Jesus said to them, "Amen, I say to you that

135

you who have followed me, in the new age, when the Son of Man is seated on his throne of glory, will yourselves sit on twelve thrones, judging the twelve tribes of Israel. [29] And everyone who has given up houses or brothers or sisters or father or mother or children or lands for the sake of my name will receive a hundred times more, and will inherit eternal life. [30] But many who are first will be last, and the last will be first."

The third passage in this chapter recounts the tale of the rich young man who desired to follow Jesus (19:16-30). Notice that he initiates the conversation with Jesus by respectfully asking a question: "Teacher, what good must I do to gain eternal life?" (v. 16) The use of the address "teacher" is courteous, but for Matthew it also implies a lack of understanding of Jesus' true nature. It appears almost exclusively on the lips of Jesus' enemies (cf. 8:19; 9:11; 12:38; 17:24; 22:16,24,36). Jesus' response sends him back to some of the primary command-ments of Jewish law, part of the famous "ten commandments" (vv. 17-19). Jesus acknowledges, in essence, the validity of the ten commandments. The young man's rejoinder, however, that he adheres already to these divine precepts, leads Jesus to issue the extra call: "If you wish to be perfect, go sell what you have and give to [the] poor, and you will have treasure in heaven. Then come, follow me" (v. 21). What a disappointment it must have been, for the young man had been expecting a commenda-tion for his achievements. Instead Jesus raises the bar a bit higher; he offers him an even bigger challenge. If you want really to be my disciple, give your belongings to the poor and focus your attention solely on the kingdom of God. Get rid of all the incidentals that distract one from the essentials. Jesus issues him the classic call to discipleship (cf. 4:19); he only needs to respond.

The young man's subsequent departure after his sad reaction to Jesus' invitation prompts Jesus to give the third challenging teaching in this chapter about discipleship (vv. 23-30).

Possessions of all kinds detract from the single-minded devotion to God's kingdom and God's values that Jesus expects of his followers. His astonished disciples again cry out in frustration, "Who then can be saved?" (v. 25) Jesus assures them, as he has elsewhere, that it may seem impossible from a strictly human perspective, but from God's perspective all things are possible (v. 26; cf. 16:23). This does not seem to ease the disciples' anxiety, for Peter, ever their bold spokesman in Matthew, ventures to ask what discipleship will hold for them, since they have given up so much to follow Jesus. Jesus is not shy in his response. He lists the very essence of many people's securities: houses, brothers, sisters, father, mother, children, lands—all these are on the chopping block for the true disciple (v. 29). In other words, discipleship means abandoning everything we hold dear in this life in order to invest ourselves fully in the life that will never end.

Just how literal are we to take this vision of Jesus? At the heart of this discussion is the meaning of the word "perfect" (v. 21, *teleios;* cf. 5:48). Discipleship is not merely a matter of enlisting. Even less is it a matter of justifying one's own actions and highlighting one's own achievements, as the young man attempted to do. It means being entirely goal-oriented, perfect in the sense that one never sits back on one's laurels and feels accomplished. In this life there is always more to do to promote the message of Jesus. Being perfect does not mean having no faults or shortcomings. Nor does it promote the scourge of perfectionism, the insatiable thirst to have everything just right. Rather, it means relying more on God's grace to push us further along the path of perfection and never being fully satisfied with how far we have come.

Pope John Paul II made eloquent use of this passage in his encyclical, *Veritatis Splendor* (The Splendor of Truth). The story is the inspiration for his long teaching on morality. He emphasizes that morality and Christian faith go together, that the ten commandments retain a universal validity useful for moral teaching, and that human freedom is intimately bound to the search for truth. The story of the rich young man illustrates appropriately the desire for moral maturity that can only be found in Christ. This story thus receives new life in a contemporary call to a renewed commitment to an ethical life.

In three short passages in this chapter, Jesus has reiterated the basic vision he inaugurated in the Sermon on the Mount. Discipleship will not be an easy matter. It entails hardship and self-denial. It requires constant striving after that which eludes us and a willingness to forgo even the most basic possessions that provide happiness, such as family, home, friends, status, and wealth. The point of the chapter is not to discourage the disciples but to make them more realistic, or perhaps I should say, more idealistic. We cannot accomplish the goal alone. God can help us achieve this vision, but we must be willing to belong to a new family that strives to live in ways that others in this world deem foolish or impossible.

The Workers in the Vineyard (20:1-16)

[1] "The kingdom of heaven is like a landowner who went out at dawn to hire laborers for his vineyard. [2] After agreeing with them for the usual daily wage, he sent them into his vineyard. [3] Going out about nine o'clock, he saw others standing idle in the marketplace, [4] and he said to them, 'You too go into my vineyard, and I will give you what is just.' [5] So they went off. [And] he went out again around noon, and around three o'clock, and did likewise. [6] Going out about five o'clock, he found others standing around, and said to them, 'Why do you stand here idle all day?' [7] They answered, 'Because no one has hired us.' He said to them, 'You too go into my vineyard.' [8] When it was evening the owner of the vineyard said to his foreman, 'Summon the laborers and give them their pay, beginning with the last and ending with the first.' [9] When those who had started about five o'clock came, each received the usual daily wage. [10] So when the first came, they thought that they would receive more, but each of them also got the usual wage. [11] And on receiving it they grumbled against the

landowner, [12] saying, 'These last ones worked only one hour, and you have made them equal to us, who bore the day's burden and the heat.' [13] He said to one of them in reply, 'My friend, I am not cheating you. Did you not agree with me for the usual daily wage? [14] Take what is yours and go. What if I wish to give this last one the same as you? [15] [Or] am I not free to do as I wish with my own money? Are you envious because I am generous?' [16] Thus, the last will be first, and the first will be last."

The provocative teaching of chapter 19 leads to further challenging words in the next. Chapter 20 contains four scenes that build upon the understanding of discipleship expounded above. The first is an extended parable (vv. 1-16), followed by the third prediction of the passion and resurrection (vv. 17-19), and then succeeded by the request of the mother of Zebedee's sons (vv. 20-28), and the plea of the two blind men at Jericho (vv. 29-34). Each passage subtly reinforces Jesus' understanding of the challenge of discipleship.

The parable of the workers in the vineyard (vv. 1-16), which is unique to Matthew's Gospel, continues Jesus' teaching on discipleship by emphasizing that the master is generous in his treatment of those who answer his call to work in his vineyard. The parable is framed by the line that ends the previous passage about the rich young man and is repeated, in reverse order, at the end of the parable: The last shall be first and the first shall be last (19:30; 20:16). The parable itself is another "kingdom" parable, explaining in parabolic fashion what God's reign is like. The comparison is with a landowner who hires a group of workers for his vineyard at 9 A.M., another group at noon, a third group at 3 P.M., and a final group at 5 P.M. Gathering them together in the evening to distribute their wages, the master has the foreman pay the workers, beginning in unusual fashion with the last hired and concluding with the first group hired. To the latter's surprise, everyone received a full day's wage, no matter how many or how few hours they had worked. Those hired first accuse the master of cheating them, but he defends his generosity and the fact that the first group had agreed to a day's wage anyway.

As with so many parables, the situation seems ludicrous at first. From a strictly human vantage point, it does not seem fair. Why should those who worked only a couple of hours get the same wage as those who bore the heat of the day? But then, the kingdom of God does not operate on our principles of justice. The teaching revolves around the reversal of first and last and the fact that, what is most important is not *when* one chooses to answer Jesus' call to discipleship, but *if* one chooses to follow Jesus at all. The juxtaposition of the images of first and last call attention to the incredible generosity of God in dealing with all those who work in the vineyard (19:30; 20:8,16). Being a member of God's kingdom is not a reward for work accomplished but a gift freely given to those who surrender to God's will.

Passion-Resurrection Prediction (20:17-28)

[17] As Jesus was going up to Jerusalem, he took the twelve [disciples] aside by themselves, and said to them on the way, [18] "Behold, we are going up to Jerusalem, and the Son of Man will be handed over to the chief priests and the scribes, and they will condemn him to death, [19] and hand him over to the Gentiles to be mocked and scourged and crucified, and he will be raised on the third day."

[20] Then the mother of the sons of Zebedee approached him with her sons and did him homage, wishing to ask him for something. [21] He said to her, "What do you wish?" She answered him, "Command that these two sons of mine sit, one at your right and the other at your left, in your kingdom." [22] Jesus said in reply, "You do not know what you are asking. Can you drink the cup that I am going to drink?" They said to him, "We can." [23] He replied, "My cup you will indeed drink, but to sit at my right and at my left (, this) is not mine to give but is for those for whom it has been prepared by my Father."

²⁴When the ten heard this, they became indignant at the two brothers. ²⁵But Jesus summoned them and said, "You know that the rulers of the Gentiles lord it over them, and the great ones make their authority over them felt. ²⁶But it shall not be so among you. Rather, whoever wishes to be great among you shall be your servant; ²⁷whoever wishes to be first among you shall be your slave. ²⁸Just so, the Son of Man did not come to be served but to serve and to give his life as a ransom for many."

On the heels of this parabolic vision is the third reminder, in the form of a passion-resurrection prediction about Jesus, that servanthood requires suffering (vv. 17-19). It is the most explicit of the three predictions (cf. 16:21; 17:22-23), containing the basic elements of Jesus' passion that is soon to be recounted in Matthew's story. Note the succession of explicit actions: going up to Jerusalem → handed over to chief priests and scribes → condemned to death → handed over to the Gentiles → mocked → scourged → crucified → raised on the third day. This terse summary of the passion and resurrection of Jesus paradoxically falls on deaf ears, for immediately following it is the third scene in the chapter where the mother of Zebedee's sons tries to obtain a significant place for her children in the future kingdom (20:20-28). When will they learn that the kingdom of heaven is not about achieving a rank but being a servant of all the others?

Perhaps we should not be too hard on this mother who, as any good mother would, seeks only the best for her children. She wants her sons to flank Jesus, one on the left and one on the right. She does not realize that, ironically, these are not places of honor but of intense sacrifice (27:38). Yet in the context of this section of Matthew, the teaching about the true nature of following Jesus is being reiterated with force just prior to the dramatic entry of Jesus into Jerusalem to accept his fate as God's Son. Jesus strongly emphasizes that service is what the community of disciples should be about. Unlike Gentile rulers, unlike those in authority, Jesus' followers are to be servant and slave (20:25-27; cf. 10:24-25). When the sons of Zebedee rather facilely indicate that they can "drink the same cup" as Jesus (i.e., experience the same fate), they really don't know what they are saying (20:22). In the time of testing, the disciples, all of them, will show their true mettle. They will betray, deny and desert their master. Words flow easier than deeds when it comes to asserting servanthood. Only Jesus, as Son of Man, has the stamina truly to serve by offering his own life as ransom (20:28).

The Two Blind Men (20:29-34)

[29] As they left Jericho, a great crowd followed him. [30] Two blind men were sitting by the roadside, and when they heard that Jesus was passing by, they cried out, "[Lord,] Son of David, have pity on us!" [31] The crowd warned them to be silent, but they called out all the more, "Lord, Son of David, have pity on us!" [32] Jesus stopped and called them and said, "What do you want me to do for you?" [33] They answered him, "Lord, let our eyes be opened." [34] Moved with pity, Jesus touched their eyes. Immediately they received their sight, and followed him.

Just how effective Jesus is at being servant is illustrated again in the next story, the last healing story of the Gospel. The cure of the two blind men on the way out of Jericho climaxes these two chapters on discipleship in a fashion that connects Jesus' own mission as God's saving, servant-son with that of his followers (20:29-34). The two blind men by the roadside cry out respectfully to Jesus as "Lord, Son of David" (vv. 30,31) and ask to be healed of their blindness. Jesus responds as a good shepherd to needy flock. He is "moved with pity" and cures them by his healing touch. They, in turn, "follow" him and thereby show that they have become his disciples at a crucial juncture as he is about to enter Jerusalem. This brief miracle

142

story unites christological themes with ecclesiological themes at a critical moment in the story. Jesus remains true to his identity as God's Son (in David's line) to use his miraculous powers to effect healing. The result, ironically, is to create two disciples in the face of the lack of proper response of his own chosen ones. They follow willingly as he trudges toward Jerusalem and his inevitable fate.

The next three chapters (ch. 21–23) should be viewed together. They largely involve Jerusalem and the Temple. Between the entrance of Jesus into Jerusalem and its environs (21:1) and leaving the Temple (24:1) is a series of events and teachings that prepare for the dramatic conclusion of the story of Jesus. Jesus' confrontations in these three chapters with Jerusalem, the Temple and its leaders set the stage for a final discourse on the end times (24:1–25:46) and the climactic story of Jesus' passion, death and resurrection. These chapters set in Jerusalem escalate the controversy between Jesus and his opponents that has been building throughout the Gospel. It is ultimately a confrontation between good and evil, between God and Satan, between true authority and trumped up power. The first two chapters (ch. 21–22) set forth the controversy by means of several prophetic events and teachings revolving around Jesus' identity and authority. These climax in a powerful chapter that excoriates the failure of the Jewish leaders and issues a final lament over Jerusalem. We will examine each of these sections briefly in some detail.

Jesus' Entry into Jerusalem (21:1-11)

[1] When they drew near Jerusalem and came to Bethphage on the Mount of Olives, Jesus sent two disciples, [2] saying to them, "Go into the village opposite you, and immediately you will find an ass tethered, and a colt with her. Untie them and bring them here to me. [3] And if anyone should say anything to you, reply, 'The master has need of them.' Then

he will send them at once." ⁴This happened so that what had been spoken through the prophet might be fulfilled:

⁵ "Say to daughter Zion,
'Behold, your king comes to you,
meek and riding on an ass, and on a colt,
the foal of a beast of burden.'"

⁶The disciples went and did as Jesus had ordered them. ⁷They brought the ass and the colt and laid their cloaks over them, and he sat upon them. ⁸The very large crowd spread their cloaks on the road, while others cut branches from the trees and strewed them on the road. ⁹The crowds preceding him and those following kept crying out and saying:

"Hosanna to the Son of David;
blessed is he who comes in the name of the Lord;
hosanna in the highest."

¹⁰ And when he entered Jerusalem the whole city was shaken and asked, "Who is this?" ¹¹And the crowds replied, "This is Jesus the prophet, from Nazareth in Galilee."

Chapter 21 begins with the preparations for Jesus' triumphal entry into Jerusalem and his visit to the Temple (21:1-17). Jesus knows prophetically how he is to go about this entrance and he gives detailed instructions to the disciples to fetch a humble beast of burden (an ass) for the event (21:2,7). As was done in much of the infancy narrative, Matthew accompanies this elaborate gesture with a prophetic fulfillment citation (v. 4; a clumsy rendering of Zechariah 9:9). Jesus' actions are still being guided by God's word. Despite his meek and humble demeanor (v. 5), the crowds hail him appropriately as Son of David, but he is also more (12:42). Just as his birth caused deep consternation in all Jerusalem (2:3), so his entrance shakes up the whole city (21:10; literally the root for *seismos* "earthquake"; cf. 8:24; 27:54; 28:2,4). A further connection is made to Jesus' origins by the question that the city poses: "Who is this?" The response of the crowds, that Jesus is a prophet from Galilee, is correct but only partly so, for he is much, much more (12:41). Jesus' entry into Jerusalem, the holy city, is the first of three prophetic actions Jesus performs.

Cleansing of the Temple (21:12-17)

[12] Jesus entered the temple area and drove out all those engaged in selling and buying there. He overturned the tables of the money changers and the seats of those who were selling doves. [13] And he said to them, "It is written:

'My house shall be a house of prayer,'

but you are making it a den of thieves."

[14] The blind and the lame approached him in the temple area, and he cured them. [15] When the chief priests and the scribes saw the wondrous things he was doing, and the children crying out in the temple area, "Hosanna to the Son of David," they were indignant [16] and said to him, "Do you hear what they are saying?" Jesus said to them, "Yes; and have you never read the text, 'Out of the mouths of infants and nurslings you have brought forth praise'?" [17] And leaving them, he went out of the city to Bethany, and there he spent the night.

Jesus immediately enters the Temple and begins to exert his authority over it by expelling those who have corrupted it with commerce (21:12-13). This is the second prophetic gesture. His actions and his quotation from the Scriptures about the Temple as a "house of prayer" that has been turned into a "den of thieves" (v. 13; Is 56:7; Jer 7:11) evoke the image of an authoritative prophet whose goal is to cleanse Israel of its sinfulness and restore faithfulness to the Temple and its leadership. This image of a powerful, and justifiably angry prophet, is balanced by the accompanying tender scene of the blind and lame approaching Jesus to be cured. Meanwhile children (little ones again) acclaim him as "Son of David," and to silence his opponents who complain about this, Jesus quotes a messianic psalm that says, "Out of the mouths of infants and nurslings, you have brought forth praise" (v. 16; cf. Ps 8:3). The Word of God continues to direct and interpret the fate of this humble messiah. Thus Jesus, as he enters the holy city of Jerusalem, is both fiery prophet and merciful, healing servant in the line of David. Both images, however, aggravate the Jewish leadership.

The Fig Tree (21:18-22)

[18] When he was going back to the city in the morning, he was hungry. [19] Seeing a fig tree by the road, he went over to it, but found nothing on it except leaves. And he said to it, "May no fruit ever come from you again." And immediately the fig tree withered. [20] When the disciples saw this, they were amazed and said, "How was it that the fig tree withered immediately?" [21] Jesus said to them in reply, "Amen, I say to you, if you have faith and do not waver, not only will you do what has been done to the fig tree, but even if you say to this mountain, 'Be lifted up and thrown into the sea,' it will be done. [22] Whatever you ask for in prayer with faith, you will receive."

The next scene may seem curious but is the third prophetic act that Jesus performs in Jerusalem, the cursing of the fig tree (vv. 18-22). The fig tree was a widely known and useful tree in Israel. It could also be a symbol of peace and tranquility (see Mi 4:4). In this context, however, Jesus' cursing of it because of the lack of fruit symbolizes the fruitlessness of the Temple and its leaders (cf. 3:8-10; 7:17-19; 12:33). They are unable to provide the proper leadership, and they are doomed. The withered fig presages the destruction of Jerusalem, the Temple, and all associated with it (see 21:43). Matthew, however, also makes this prophetic action into an object lesson for the disciples. Their amazement at the immediate effect of Jesus' curse leads to a teaching. Jesus informs them again of the need for unwavering faith in order to have one's prayers answered (vv. 21-22; cf. 17:19-20). He assures them, "Whatever you ask for in prayer with faith, you will receive" (v. 22). These words provide direction to disciples in every age. Prayer and faith go together. They are especially pertinent in times of trial and tribulation. The

146

negative judgment against the Temple paradoxically provides a positive instruction for the new "temple," the community of Jesus.

Confrontation between Jesus and the Chief Priests (21:23-27)

> [23] When he had come into the temple area, the chief priests and the elders of the people approached him as he was teaching and said, "By what authority are you doing these things? And who gave you this authority?" [24] Jesus said to them in reply, "I shall ask you one question, and if you answer it for me, then I shall tell you by what authority I do these things. [25] Where was John's baptism from? Was it of heavenly or of human origin?" They discussed this among themselves and said, "If we say 'Of heavenly origin,' he will say to us, 'Then why did you not believe him?' [26] But if we say, 'Of human origin,' we fear the crowd, for they all regard John as a prophet." [27] So they said to Jesus in reply, "We do not know." He himself said to them, "Neither shall I tell you by what authority I do these things."

The three prophetic actions lead to an intense confrontation between Jesus and the chief priests and elders of the people (21:23-27). They recognize that his deeds possess an incredible authority (remember also the reaction to his teaching, 7:29), but they query whence it comes. In response, Jesus poses a question to them about the authority of John the Baptist. They realize that they, who have intended to trap Jesus with his response, are themselves caught in a trap. If they say John's authority is from God, then Jesus could ask why they did not believe in him. If they say the opposite, they risk the ire of the people who thought of John as a prophet. They refuse to answer, and Jesus refuses likewise to address their question. The issue of Jesus' authority, however, which has been a dominant motif throughout the Gospel tied to his identity, will remain just below the surface of the remaining chapters. Addressing

147

that question is not a matter of insincere human investigation but of authentic faith.

Three Parables (21:28–22:14)

This failed attempt by the Jewish leaders to probe Jesus' authority leads to three parables that relate to the three earlier prophetic gestures. Each of them has allegorical elements typical of Matthew, and each concerns aspects of the failure of the Jewish leaders in their obligations. The three are:

1) the parable of the two sons (21:28-32)
2) the parable of the wicked tenants (21:33-46)
3) the parable of the wedding feast (22:1-14).

> [28] "What is your opinion? A man had two sons. He came to the first and said, 'Son, go out and work in the vineyard today.' [29] He said in reply, 'I will not,' but afterwards he changed his mind and went. [30] The man came to the other son and gave the same order. He said in reply, 'Yes, sir,' but did not go. [31] Which of the two did his father's will?" They answered, "The first." Jesus said to them, "Amen, I say to you, tax collectors and prostitutes are entering the kingdom of God before you. [32] When John came to you in the way of righteousness, you did not believe him; but tax collectors and prostitutes did. Yet even when you saw that, you did not later change your minds and believe him."

The first parable is set in a vineyard, a favorite symbol of Israel (Is 5:1-7), and is intended to address the leaders' failure to answer Jesus' question about John the Baptist (see v. 32). The owner had two sons whom he asked to work in his vineyard. One said "no" but later changed his mind and went; the other said "yes" but never went. When Jesus asks which one actually did his father's will, the Jewish leaders correctly point to the first. Jesus then reveals the essential message. Sinners will enter the kingdom before the Jewish leaders! Prostitutes and tax collectors are like the first son, but the leaders are like the second son. They ignored John's "way of righteousness" whereas common sinners believed in him (v. 32). For us the message is also clear. Authentic faith does not rest in going through the motions of pious practices but in utter trust in God and God's righteous messengers. The point becomes even clearer and more trenchant in the second parable.

³³ "Hear another parable. There was a landowner who planted a vineyard, put a hedge around it, dug a wine press in it, and built a tower. Then he leased it to tenants and went on a journey. ³⁴ When vintage time drew near, he sent his servants to the tenants to obtain his produce. ³⁵ But the tenants seized the servants and one they beat, another they killed, and a third they stoned. ³⁶ Again he sent other servants, more numerous than the first ones, but they treated them in the same way. ³⁷ Finally, he sent his son to them, thinking, 'They will respect my son.' ³⁸ But when the tenants saw the son, they said to one another, 'This is the heir. Come, let us kill him and acquire his inheritance.' ³⁹ They seized him, threw him out of the vineyard, and killed him. ⁴⁰ What will the owner of the vineyard do to those tenants when he comes?" ⁴¹ They answered him, "He will put those wretched men to a wretched death and lease his vineyard to other tenants who will give him the produce at the proper times." ⁴² Jesus said to them, "Did you never read in the scriptures:

'The stone that the builders rejected

has become the cornerstone;

by the Lord has this been done,

and it is wonderful in our eyes'?

⁴³ Therefore, I say to you, the kingdom of God will be taken away from you and given to a people that will produce its fruit. ⁴⁴ [The one who falls on this stone will be dashed to pieces; and it will crush anyone on whom it falls.]" ⁴⁵ When the chief priests and the Pharisees heard his parables, they knew that he was speaking about them. ⁴⁶ And although they

were attempting to arrest him, they feared the crowds, for they regarded him as a prophet.

The parable of the wicked tenants is also set in a vineyard and provides a climactic moment to the confrontation between Jesus and the Jewish leadership in Jerusalem (21:33-46). This well-known parable is filled with allegorical elements that I will explain by means of parentheses. Three sets of servants (=prophets) are sent to harvest the vineyard (=the faith of Israel), but they are maltreated by the tenants who lease it and vainly hope to wrest it from the owner. The tenants cruelly abuse the servants with the result that the owner (=God, the Father) sends his own son (=Jesus) to obtain his produce. The tenants throw him outside the vineyard (=Jerusalem) and kill him (=crucifixion). Ironically, Jesus tricks the Jewish leaders who hear this parable into pronouncing with their own lips the judgment against the wicked tenants. The owner "will put those wretched men to a wretched death and lease his vineyard to other tenants . . ." (v. 41). Jesus then adds another Scripture quotation (from messianic Psalm 110) and pronounces the judgment that the "kingdom of God" will be taken away and given to a "people" (=the Church) that will produce fruit (=live righteously). The wording is precise and unmistakable. The Jewish leadership realizes the parable is paradoxically all about them (v. 45), but their attempt to arrest Jesus is thwarted again by their fear of the crowd.

Typical of allegorical parables, this one has some fluid images that change in the course of the story (e.g., the meaning of the vineyard fluctuates). However, one cannot doubt its function in Matthew's story. For Matthew and his community, the Jewish leaders failed miserably in their obligations. They had squandered the trust God placed in them. The kingdom of God could no longer rest on the heritage of Israel, but was now entrusted to a new people (literally, *ethnos*, "Gentile" or "nation") that would produce fruit. Matthew's community recognized their religious indebtedness to Judaism, but the obstinate failure of the religious leaders to fulfill their duties produced an irreparable rupture in the status quo. In Jesus, God had acted definitively to provide a new path to righteousness, prepared for by John the Baptist. The constant rejection of this new path by those who should have been the first to embrace it would necessitate casting the net much wider. Sinners would enter God's kingdom ahead of the self-righteous. Gentiles would accept God's message with zeal rather than God's own chosen people.

22:1 Jesus again in reply spoke to them in parables, saying, 2 "The kingdom of heaven may be likened to a king who gave a wedding feast for his son. 3 He dispatched his servants to summon the invited guests to the feast, but they refused to come. 4 A second time he sent other servants, saying, 'Tell those invited: "Behold, I have prepared my banquet, my calves and fattened cattle are killed, and everything is ready; come to the feast."' 5 Some ignored the invitation and went away, one to his farm, another to his business. 6 The rest laid hold of his servants, mistreated them, and killed them. 7 The king was enraged and sent his troops, destroyed those murderers, and burned their city. 8 Then he said to his servants, 'The feast is ready, but those who were invited were not worthy to come. 9 Go out, therefore, into the main roads and invite to the feast whomever you find.' 10 The servants went out into the streets and gathered all they found, bad and good alike, and the hall was filled with guests. 11 But when the king came in to meet the guests he saw a man there not dressed in a wedding garment. 12 He said to him, 'My friend, how is it that you came in here without a wedding garment?' But he was reduced to silence. 13 Then the king said to his attendants, 'Bind his hands and feet, and cast him into the darkness outside, where there will be wailing and grinding of teeth.' 14 Many are invited, but few are chosen."

The third parable brings home this message of the transfer of membership in this new reality by the parable of the wedding feast (22:1-14). Marriage was a traditional biblical symbol of the covenantal relationship between God and God's people (Is 54:5; Hos 2:1-9). The wedding banquet also provided a symbol of the peace and harmony that would come one day in God's kingdom (Is 25:6). In this parable Jesus uses the image allegorically to represent the shift that has come about by Israel's failure to read the signs of the times. Coupled with the previous parable, it also explains the destruction of Jerusalem. The parable concerns a king (=God) who gave a wedding banquet in honor of his son (=Jesus). He dispatched his servants (=prophets) to invite his guests (=Israel), but all refused or were too busy to attend. So he destroyed their city (=Jerusalem) and invited all the outcasts he could find (= sinners of all stripes). One man, however, lacked a wedding garment (=repentance for sin, conversion) and was cast out into the darkness. Jesus concludes, "Many are invited, but few are chosen" (v. 14). Again the lesson is rather transparent. Nominal religion is not sufficient to get into God's kingdom. Many who think they belong are actually too preoccupied with matters of lesser importance. The dregs of the earth who are consequently invited must properly prepare themselves for the banquet. They must repent and lead righteous lives, else they will suffer the consequences of judgment (cf. 8:12; 13:42,50, etc.). Though God issues the invitation broadly, the number who will actually be found worthy is smaller than one would expect or hope. Faith is a difficult road to follow, and we should not be deceived that it will be easy.

Plotting Against Jesus (22:15-46)

[15] Then the Pharisees went off and plotted how they might entrap him in speech. [16] They sent their disciples to him, with the Herodians, saying, "Teacher, we know that you are a truthful man and that you teach the way of God in accordance with the truth. And you are not concerned with anyone's opinion, for you do not regard a person's status. [17] Tell us, then, what is your opinion: Is it lawful to pay the

census tax to Caesar or not?" [18] Knowing their malice, Jesus said, "Why are you testing me, you hypocrites? [19] Show me the coin that pays the census tax." Then they handed him the Roman coin. [20] He said to them, "Whose image is this and whose inscription?" [21] They replied, "Caesar's." At that he said to them, "Then repay to Caesar what belongs to Caesar and to God what belongs to God." [22] When they heard this they were amazed, and leaving him they went away.

At the conclusion of the three parables, the Pharisees depart to refine their plot against Jesus (22:15). Notice that Matthew's designation for the Jewish leaders throughout this section of the Gospel is not always consistent. The reason is that he conceives of all the Jewish leadership as evil and allied against Jesus. In this next scene the Pharisees send some of their own disciples, along with some Herodians, to try to trap Jesus (22:15-22). This is the first of three successively futile attempts in this section to ensnare Jesus in controversy. The first topic is payment of taxes. They question Jesus on whether it is legitimate to pay the Roman census tax (v. 17). Knowing their evil intention, he solicits a coin with Caesar's image on it. The conversation leads to Jesus' famous line: "Then repay to Caesar what belongs to Caesar and to God what belongs to God" (v. 21). Jesus beats them again at their own game. He avoids answering the question directly and leaves them amazed. For much of the history of interpretation, Jesus' saying has been used to validate the separation of Church and state or of religion and politics. That is probably going beyond what the text can bear. Jesus' response permits the payment of tax yet does not validate Roman rule over Israel at a time when that was highly controversial. He thus avoids either a seditious remark or one that aggravates Jewish nationalistic feelings. More to the point is the necessity of knowing what God ultimately requires of us. Jesus' response emphasizes the failure of the Jewish leaders to discern where their ultimate obligations lie. They are so busy trying to trap Jesus that they can scarcely distinguish

153

between civil and religious obligations, let alone understand God's will. They depart empty-handed.

[23] On that day Sadducees approached him, saying that there is no resurrection. They put this question to him, [24] saying, "Teacher, Moses said, 'If a man dies without children, his brother shall marry his wife and raise up descendants for his brother.' [25] Now there were seven brothers among us. The first married and died and, having no descendants, left his wife to his brother. [26] The same happened with the second and the third, through all seven. [27] Finally the woman died. [28] Now at the resurrection, of the seven, whose wife will she be? For they all had been married to her." [29] Jesus said to them in reply, "You are misled because you do not know the scriptures or the power of God. [30] At the resurrection they neither marry nor are given in marriage but are like the angels in heaven. [31] And concerning the resurrection of the dead, have you not read what was said to you by God, [32] 'I am the God of Abraham, the God of Isaac, and the God of Jacob'? He is not the God of the dead but of the living." [33] When the crowds heard this, they were astonished at his teaching.

Another set of opponents, the Sadducees, try their hand at entrapment "on that day" (22:23-33). Their question concerns the resurrection. We should remember that, in comparison to the Pharisees, they opposed the notion of resurrection. They try to show the silliness of the idea by hypothesizing a case wherein seven brothers consecutively marry the same woman upon the death of each successive brother. The custom of passing on a widow to one's brother-in-law was, in fact, permitted in the law (Dt 25:5-6). It is called a Levirate marriage, and its purpose was to ensure that the deceased man's family lineage continued. Again Jesus sees through their plot. His response castigates their failure to know either the scriptures or God's power. At the resurrection, marriage will be irrelevant, for people will live "like the angels in heaven" (v. 30). This cryptic phrase apparently means that human sexual relationships will be transcended in the resurrected life.

We should not concern ourselves so much with the details of the next life as with what is asked of us in this life. God is a God of the living and not the dead (v. 32). This statement does not negate the importance of the resurrection in Christian faith but puts it in proper perspective. We should not worry ourselves with excessive speculations about the life to come but about how to live the life we are given here on earth. We trust ultimately in God's power to conquer death and to assure eternal life without needing to know the details of what resurrected life will be like. In an age fascinated with angels, the occult, and conceptions of life after death, we should take note of this teaching. Movies may fill our imaginations with all kinds of nostalgic images about the afterlife, but they do not usually preach the gospel.

[34] When the Pharisees heard that he had silenced the Sadducees, they gathered together, [35] and one of them (a scholar of the law) tested him by asking, [36] "Teacher, which commandment in the law is the greatest?" [37] He said to him, "You shall love the Lord, your God, with all your heart, with all your soul, and with all your mind. [38] This is the greatest and the first commandment. [39] The second is like it: You shall love your neighbor as yourself. [40] The whole law and the prophets depend on these two commandments."

[41] While the Pharisees were gathered together, Jesus questioned them, [42] saying, "What is your opinion about the Messiah? Whose son is he?" They replied, "David's." [43] He said to them, "How, then, does David, inspired by the Spirit, call him 'lord,' saying:

[44] 'The Lord said to my lord,
"Sit at my right hand
until I place your enemies under your feet" '?

[45] If David calls him 'lord,' how can he be his son?" [46] No one was able to answer him a word, nor from that day on did anyone dare to ask him any more questions.

The result of the controversy is that the Sadducees are silenced (22:34), and the Pharisees return for a final controversy, divided into two parts (22:34-40 and 22:41-46). A Pharisaic lawyer first attempts to test Jesus by asking which commandment of the Law is the greatest. Maybe it takes a lawyer's mind to conceive such a question. Ingeniously, Jesus takes two parts of the Torah and combines them into a single statement that digests all the commandments into two: love of God (Dt 6:5) and love of neighbor (Lv 19:18). In one fell swoop Jesus' teaching encompasses the dual primary obligations of human existence. These commandments cover the vertical and horizontal dimensions of love. To love God with all our being and to love our neighbor as ourselves summarizes well the essence of Christian morality. The whole Law and the prophets depend on these two principles (v. 40).

Jesus may not have been alone is singling out special commandments, for the rabbinic tradition recognized that the 613 commandments of the Torah were not all of equal value. There was a need to prioritize them. Other rabbis digested the Law into various summaries. Jesus does so in an efficient manner. Interestingly, the second commandment, love of neighbor, is repeated in two other different contexts in Matthew (5:43; 19:19). Perhaps this indicates just how difficult this commandment is. I remember a Peanuts cartoon in which one of the characters touts his ability to love. I paraphrase his statement this way: "I love humankind. It's people I can't stand." Jesus must have understood just how difficult love of neighbor is. Loving the God we cannot see is easier than loving the people we do see—until we realize that loving people is inextricably linked to loving God. Taken together, Jesus' threefold teaching in Matthew about love of neighbor has three distinctive elements:

1) our neighbor includes even our enemies (5:43-44)
2) love of neighbor is part of the general morality of God's Law (19:18-19)

3) love of neighbor must be seen side-by-side with love of God (22:37-39).

The text does not describe a response on the part of the lawyer who asked the question. Jesus' summary of the Law speaks for itself.

The second part of this final controversy involves the identity of the messiah (22:41-46). Jesus becomes the interrogator. He inquires of the Pharisees about whose son the messiah must be, to which they properly reply, "David's." Then, quoting scripture, Jesus wonders how the messiah can be both "son" and "lord" (v. 45; Ps 110:1). They demonstrate Jesus' earlier accusations that they do not know the Scriptures, for they are unable to respond. In essence, Matthew has brought the question of Jesus' identity and authority full circle with this confrontation. Jesus is both David's Son and Lord. Only he has the authority to heal and to judge granted to him by his heavenly Father. Through these two chapters of controversy, in deed and in word, he has confirmed for the reader that he is the messiah, the long-awaited one. He has silenced his enemies (22:46), and the situation leads to Jesus' final, harsh condemnation of the failure of the Jewish religious leadership.

The Hypocrisy of the Scribes and the Pharisees (23:1-36)

[1] Then Jesus spoke to the crowds and to his disciples, [2] saying, "The scribes and the Pharisees have taken their seat on the chair of Moses. [3] Therefore, do and observe all things whatsoever they tell you, but do not follow their example. For they preach but they do not practice. [4] They tie up heavy burdens [hard to carry] and lay them on people's shoulders, but they will not lift a finger to move them. [5] All their works are performed to be seen. They widen their phylacteries and lengthen their tassels. [6] They love places of honor at banquets, seats of honor in synagogues, [7] greetings in marketplaces, and the salutation 'Rabbi.' [8] As for you, do not be called 'Rabbi.'

You have but one teacher, and you are all brothers. ⁹Call no one on earth your father; you have but one Father in heaven. ¹⁰Do not be called 'Master'; you have but one master, the Messiah. ¹¹The greatest among you must be your servant. ¹²Whoever exalts himself will be humbled; but whoever humble himself will be exalted."

Chapter 23 brings this section of controversies to a dramatic conclusion. A lengthy speech summarizes the ultimate failure of the Jewish leaders and leads Jesus to lament the fate of Jerusalem. The chapter thus divides into two unequal parts: 23:1-36 and 23:37-39. The first part of this chapter can itself be divided into two sections. The first summarizes the role of the Jewish leaders in general fashion (vv. 1-12). The second lists a series of seven "woes" that illustrate their failures (vv. 13-36).

The first part addresses two general issues. One concerns the need to respect the authority of the Jewish leaders because of the position they hold vis-à-vis the Law. Attached to this admonition is the warning not to imitate their behavior because they do not practice what they say. The second issue is Jesus' warning against assuming titles and positions that are not appropriate for his followers. Both issues deserve some further reflection.

Do Jesus' words about respecting the scribes and Pharisees and doing "whatever they tell you" not contradict his position on them elsewhere in the Gospel? Does this statement not mitigate his condemnation of them in the rest of the chapter? The answer to these questions must be "no" but the reason may not be so easy to ascertain. The key seems to be in the word "tell" (v. 3). They can *speak* words about the Law with authority because of their position, but one should not follow their example because they are incapable of living out what they speak in their own lives. In other words, Jesus does not attack the religious institution of authoritative teachers in the line of Moses but the particular teachers who currently are unable to live concretely by their own words. Jesus bolsters his warning with examples of the abuse of their power (vv. 4-10):

- they put burdens on others and make no attempt to ease them
- they "perform" their duties publicly to be seen by others
- they adorn their garments with superfluous decorations
- they like the places of honor in public places or at public events
- they like titles of honor and respect, like "rabbi," "father" and "master."

All of these actions belie their calling. They attract attention to themselves and impose obligations on others. They also directly oppose the teaching of Jesus who calls his disciples to be humble servants (v. 12; cf. 20:26-27).

Jesus gives a second injunction about titles. He warns his disciples not to accept titles like rabbi, father, or master because only one can fulfill these titles. God alone is Father, and Jesus alone is rabbi (teacher) and master. Some fundamentalists have used this saying to oppose the Catholic practice of addressing the priest as "father," but this interpretation makes it into a generic principle taken out of context. If this were a general principle, then the practice elsewhere in the NT would be problematic. Paul, for instance, saw himself as a "father" in relation to his churches (1 Cor 4:15; Phil 2:22). Jesus' point in Matthew is that respect is something that should come from the person, not from external titles meant to impress. In the context of calling for respect of office, Jesus also warns against using one's position or its external trappings to bolster one's self-image, especially in relationship to others. In my experience, some priests (and even bishops) have been overly enamored of their office and its trappings. Clericalism is a force that should be resisted in the Church. Yet the same could be said of some non-Catholic ministers who excessively rely on their academic degrees or their ordained status; they like the title "Doctor" or "Reverend." Anyone can fall victim to the allure of title or position. Disciples are to avoid these excesses, but that is not a call to abandon all positions in the Church. Even Matthew's community had distinctive leaders with diverse roles to play (10:40-42; sages, prophets).

Both pieces of general advice, then, are meant to draw attention to true Christian leadership which is humble and service-oriented.

[13] "Woe to you, scribes and Pharisees, you hypocrites. You lock the kingdom of heaven before human beings. You do not enter yourselves, nor do you allow entrance to those trying to enter. [15] Woe to you, scribes and Pharisees, you hypocrites. You traverse sea and land to make one convert, and when that happens you make him a child of Gehenna twice as much as yourselves.

[16] "Woe to you, blind guides, who say, 'If one swears by the temple, it means nothing, but if one swears by the gold of the temple, one is obligated.' [17] Blind fools, which is greater, the gold, or the temple that made the gold sacred? [18] And you say, 'If one swears by the altar, it means nothing, but if one swears by the gift on the altar, one is obligated.' [19] You blind ones, which is greater, the gift, or the altar that makes the gift sacred? [20] One who swears by the altar swears by it and all that is upon it; [21] one who swears by the temple swears by it and by him who dwells in it; [22] one who swears by heaven swears by the throne of God and by him who is seated on it. [23] Woe to you, scribes and Pharisees, you hypocrites. You pay tithes of mint and dill and cummin, and have neglected the weightier things of the law: judgment and mercy and fidelity. [But] these you should have done, without neglecting the others. [24] Blind guides, who strain out the gnat and swallow the camel!

[25] "Woe to you, scribes and Pharisees, you hypocrites. You cleanse the outside of cup and dish, but inside they are full of

plunder and self-indulgence. [26] Blind Pharisee, cleanse first the inside of the cup, so that the outside also may be clean.

[27] "Woe to you, scribes and Pharisees, you hypocrites. You are like whitewashed tombs, which appear beautiful on the outside, but inside are full of dead men's bones and every kind of filth. [28] Even so, on the outside you appear righteous, but inside you are filled with hypocrisy and evildoing.

[29] "Woe to you, scribes and Pharisees, you hypocrites. You build the tombs of the prophets and adorn the memorials of the righteous, [30] and you say, 'If we had lived in the days of our ancestors, we would not have joined them in shedding the prophets' blood.' [31] Thus you bear witness against yourselves that you are the children of those who murdered the prophets; [32] now fill up what your ancestors measured out! [33] You serpents, you brood of vipers, how can you flee from the judgment of Gehenna? [34] Therefore, behold, I send to you prophets and wise men and scribes; some of them you will kill and crucify, some of them you will scourge in your synagogues and pursue from town to town, [35] so that there may come upon you all the righteous blood shed upon earth, from the righteous blood of Abel to the blood of Zechariah, the son of Barachiah, whom you murdered between the sanctuary and the altar. [36] Amen, I say to you, all these things will come upon this generation."

The next section lists seven woes against the Jewish leaders, representing the completeness of their failure (vv. 13-36). [Note that v. 14 is not included; it is a woe judged by scholars to be a later addition to Matthew.] A woe is an exclamation of sorrow or grief or a pronouncement of threat. It is a prophetic form of speech found in the OT (Is 5:8,11; Am 5:7,18; etc.). All of the woes in this chapter of Matthew are directed against the Jewish leaders, specifically the scribes and Pharisees, who are called various derogatory names like hypocrite, brood of vipers, and blind guides. I will outline the reasons for the woes briefly:

1) locking the kingdom of heaven (v. 13)
2) traveling widely to find converts, only to corrupt them (v. 15)
3) promoting foolish oaths at the Temple in return for offerings (vv. 16-22)
4) paying tithes on minor matters and ignoring the major demands of the Law (vv. 23-24)
5) paying attention to external details while ignoring the more important internal matters (vv. 25-26)
6) putting on external appearances while remaining corrupt internally (vv. 27-28)
7) paying nominal homage to the prophets while actually arranging their murder (vv. 29-36).

One can discern a pattern in the woes. The first three might be grouped together as offenses related to corrupting converts and preventing their proper access to God. The next three emphasize different ways in which the leaders cannot get their priorities straight. They worry about minor matters; they miss the forest for the trees. The final woe is the climax of the list. All of the leaders' failings pale in comparison to the plotting against and murder of the prophets God sent to Israel. Historically speaking, there were very few prophets actually murdered in Israel's history, although many were ridiculed and persecuted. The only prophetic example named in this text is Zechariah, son of Barachiah (Zec 1:1), but there is no biblical evidence that he was murdered. The evangelist may have confused the name with Zechariah, son of Jehoiada, who was murdered in the days of King Joash (2 Chr 24:20-22). At any rate, Matthew envisions a continual series of reprisals against the prophets throughout Israel's history. John the Baptist stands in that line, as will the disciples after Jesus himself. For Matthew, this is the worst of the offenses. It climaxes the series of woes that leads to Jesus' lament over the doomed city of Jerusalem.

Lament over Jerusalem (23:37-39)

[37] "Jerusalem, Jerusalem, you who kill the prophets and stone those sent to you, how many times I yearned to gather your children together, as a hen gathers her young under her wings, but you were unwilling! [38] Behold, your house will be abandoned, desolate. [39] I tell you, you will not see me again until you say, 'Blessed is he who comes in the name of the Lord.'"

The chapter concludes with Jesus' poignant words of lament in which he posits himself as a mother hen tenderly trying to care for wayward chicks (23:37-39). In this short passage Jesus confirms Jerusalem's sad fate because of its continual infidelity to God. He also mourns the loss of these "children." We see again the image of a tender, kind, merciful Jesus who attempts to reach out to his errant brood. Even after the stunning litany of the leaders' failures, Jesus' words reach out in sorrow to provide some measure of comfort to a recalcitrant people.

Before moving to the next section of the Gospel, we should take a moment to examine the impact of chapter 23. It is a sad fact of history that this chapter, along with some other NT materials, has been used improperly to justify anti-Semitic feelings and actions. The unremittingly strong words against the scribes and Pharisees make it seem to some that Jews throughout history are forever doomed in their stubborn adherence to the non-essentials of the Law. I offer a more balanced approach to the material with a few comments.

First, we must always remember the historical context of this material. Matthew's Gospel was composed at a time when the Romans had already destroyed Jerusalem and the Temple. All the Jewish leadership had been annihilated or fled, and the only remaining leaders were of Pharisaic background. As I said in the introduction to this commentary, I believe the evangelist and his community were in a tense relationship with the "synagogue across the street." Much of the condemnatory language directed against the Pharisees can be explained as the result of tension between Christians and Jews that built up in the wake of Jerusalem's destruction. Such tensions led to hyperbole and exaggerated enmity. The tone of the Gospel, then, is not intended for all time but reflects a particular period in history during which tempers flared beyond reasonable bounds.

A second observation is that Jesus' condemnation of the Jewish leaders' failings is not uniform. He respects the office they hold (23:2-3) and he insists that there is such a thing as a good scribe (13:52). Hypocrites can be found in any religion. First century Judaism held no patent on religious hypocrisy or on the inability to keep religious essentials in the foreground. Jesus' words of condemnation and warning can apply to any religious leaders who abuse their position. The issue now is not the Jewishness of Jesus' opponents, but anyone who fails in the standards Jesus sets forth.

Third, from this perspective, we can still mine Matthew 23 for spiritual insight if we place ourselves in the position of the Jewish leaders. What are our failings with respect to our religious attitudes and behavior? In what ways are we hypocritical, saying one thing and acting out another? Have we ever deceived others by placing undue burdens on them we would never assume for ourselves? If religion can corrupt, then authority with religion can tend to corrupt even more. Religious leaders have a particularly serious duty to be wary of their motivations and actions. Jesus' words sound a caution applicable to every age. I think of the words used at the ordination of Catholic priests: believe what you read; teach what you believe; and put into practice what you teach. This is sound advice consistent with Jesus' message. It is also a serious challenge to incarnate in daily life.

Fourth, much of the strong language reflects intra-Jewish dialogue that occurred at various times in Jewish history. First-century Judaism was a complex phenomenon. Many different groups vied for the support and attention of the populace. Arguments often developed, and tempers frequently flared. Jewish groups could be very harsh to one another. I believe that Matthew was a member of a Jewish community, albeit one who believed that Jesus was the messiah, in which intra-Jewish questions still arose, even while Gentiles had begun to adhere to the gospel message and enter the community. In consequence, Matthew should not be viewed so much as a Christian throwing stones at Jews, but as a fellow Jew and like the prophets before him, castigating the failure of his counterparts to believe in Jesus. His interpretation also provided a convenient and justifiable way to explain in hindsight why Jerusalem and the Temple were destroyed. God was now doing something entirely new in salvation history.

Destruction and Calamities (24:1-14)

[1] Jesus left the temple area and was going away, when his disciples approached him to point out the temple buildings. [2] He said to them in reply, "You see all these things, do you not? Amen, I say to you, there will not be left here a stone upon another stone that will not be thrown down." [3] As he was sitting on the Mount of Olives, the disciples approached him privately and said, "Tell us, when will this happen, and what sign will there be of your coming, and of the end of the age?" [4] Jesus said to them in reply, "See that no one deceives you. [5] For many will come in my name, saying, 'I am the Messiah,' and they will deceive many. [6] You will hear of wars and reports of wars; see that you are not alarmed, for these things must happen, but it will not yet be the end. [7] Nation will rise against nation, and kingdom against kingdom; there will be famines and earthquakes from place to place. [8] All these are the beginning of the labor pains. [9] Then they will hand you over to persecution, and they will kill you. You will be hated by all nations because of my name. [10] And then many will be led into sin; they will betray and hate one another. [11] Many false prophets will arise and deceive many; [12] and because of the increase of evildoing, the love of many will grow cold. [13] But the one who perseveres to the end will be

saved. [14] And this gospel of the kingdom will be preached throughout the world as a witness to all nations, and then the end will come."

After this dramatic confrontation with the Jewish leaders in and around Jerusalem, Jesus leaves the Temple area and proceeds to the Mount of Olives, opposite the Temple (24:1). Even today the setting on the mount of Olives is spectacular as one looks across the Kidron Valley to the old city of Jerusalem. In Jesus' day it would have also been an impressive sight to gaze upon King Herod's splendid Temple. This setting is the backdrop for the fifth and final discourse in the gospel, the so-called apocalyptic or eschatological discourse (24:1–25:46). It is appropriately named that not only because it is the last discourse of Jesus in the Gospel but also because it concerns the events that will happen in the end time, the eschaton. The first chapter of the discourse focuses on six interrelated teachings about the events of the end time (24:1-51). The second chapter has three parables that climax Jesus' teaching about the coming judgment (25:1-46).

A sevenfold outline of chapter 24 helps us to see its teaching in context:

1) the destruction of the Temple foretold (vv. 1-2)
2) the calamities that will befall the earth (vv. 3-14)
3) the great tribulation that is to come (vv. 15-28)
4) the parousia, the coming of the Son of Man in judgment (vv. 29-31)
5) the image of the fig tree (vv. 32-35)
6) the unknown day and hour (vv. 36-44)
7) the parable of the faithful and unfaithful servant (vv. 45-51).

The background of much of this material comes from the OT, in particular sections of the Book of Daniel (especially ch. 7–8). We should remember that apocalyptic thought

166

developed in post-exilic Judaism and continued to be influential in the early decades of Christianity. Apocalyptic thought developed its appeal especially in times of persecution or dire historical events. As we noted in the introduction, Matthew exhibits a strong interest in these Jewish motifs. Some of the characteristics of apocalyptic literature include:

- a strong interest in the events of the end of the world

- dualism, i.e., seeing things two-dimensionally as diametrically opposed realities

- a belief that God, in spite of appearances, is in charge of human history and will ultimately bring it to a dramatic conclusion

- a conviction that God will bring a great judgment on the earth and will vindicate the righteous and condemn the unrighteous

- a fervent call to live an ethically upright life in the face of insurmountable odds.

Some scholars have tried in recent years to minimize the influence of such apocalyptic imagery on the teaching of Jesus. They think of it as a set of superstitious beliefs that played little part in the life of the historical Jesus. In my judgment, apocalyptic thought is rooted in the teaching of both John the Baptist and Jesus, and Matthew preserves vestiges of that teaching especially in this part of the Gospel (cf. also Mk 13). Curiously, as we began a new millennium, interest in apocalyptic thought found its way into modern life. It is not simply a remnant of a bygone era but an attitude that appears now and again in history. Survivalists predicted a cataclysmic event at the turn of the millennium and stockpiled supplies to ensure their survival. Others forecasted doom because of Y2K (=year two thousand) glitches in computers, anticipating shutdowns in banking, government, industry, etc. Interest in detailing the possible events of such a turn of the ages resurrects every so often in Christian history, but Jesus' teaching in Matthew is more complex than such simplistic scenarios.

In the first scene of the discourse Jesus departs the Temple and tells his disciples that the buildings they see will soon collapse (vv. 1-2). He has already assaulted the Temple and its leadership with prophetic gestures of cleansing (21:12-13), and now he foretells the dire consequences of their failure to live out God's Law. The disciples' response is to desire to know the specifics of this prophecy, and this is the focus of the next scene (vv. 3-14). This is a natural inclination. Who wouldn't like to know in advance when some disaster will strike? Who would not want to be given the signs to look for in order to prepare for such catastrophic events? Some have read Jesus' response to their question as a blueprint of the disaster. Jesus lists some signs to watch for, such as false messiahs, wars and rumors of wars, family discord, hatred against Jesus' disciples, false prophets, an increase of evil deeds, and love growing cold (vv. 6-12). But notice how general such calamities are. They could apply at many different times of history and in many different circumstances. More importantly, Jesus exhorts his disciples not to be deceived (v. 4) and promises that the gospel will indeed be preached throughout the world (v. 14).

The Great Tribulation (24:15-44)

[15] "When you see the desolating abomination spoken of through Daniel the prophet standing in the holy place (let the reader understand), [16] then those in Judea must flee to the mountains, [17] a person on the housetop must not go down to get things out of his house, [18] a person in the field must not return to get his cloak. [19] Woe to pregnant women and nursing mothers in those days. [20] Pray that your flight not be in winter or on the Sabbath, [21] for at that time there will be great tribulation, such as has not been since the beginning of the world until now, nor ever will be. [22] And if those days had

not been shortened, no one would be saved; but for the sake of the elect they will be shortened. [23] If anyone says to you then, 'Look, here is the Messiah!' or, 'There he is!' do not believe it. [24] False messiahs and false prophets will arise, and they will perform signs and wonders so great as to deceive, if that were possible, even the elect. [25] Behold, I have told it to you beforehand. [26] So if they say to you, 'He is in the desert,' do not go out there; if they say, 'He is in the inner rooms,' do not believe it. [27] For just as lightning comes from the east and is seen as far as the west, so will the coming of the Son of Man be. [28] Wherever the corpse is, there the vultures will gather."

The next section, however, zeroes in on a specific image called the "desolating abomination" (vv. 15-28). It is an image taken from the Book of Daniel based on the historical event of 167 B.C. when the Syrian King Antiochus IV Epiphanes desecrated the Temple by erecting a statue of the pagan god, Zeus (Dn 12:11). Matthew contemporizes this historical image for his audience (the side comment in v. 15, "let the reader understand") and uses it as a prediction of the desecration of the Temple by the Romans which did, in fact, take place in A.D. 70. Matthew has already alluded to this destruction elsewhere (22:7). There follows a series of exhortations and examples that are meant to help prepare the disciples to confront the coming tribulations. Pray that the circumstances will allow time to flee (not on the Sabbath, in summer rather than winter). Watch out for false prophets and false messiahs; they will mislead you with deceptive signs. The Son of Man will come more mysteriously than that, like lightning that crisscrosses the sky from east to west (v. 27). But it will still be a day of gloom, like vultures waiting for corpses (v. 28).

Jesus' instruction is to sound a warning. It is easy to be deceived. Many times we have witnessed the forecasters of doom and gloom. Sometimes they stand at street corners with signs predicting the end of the world; sometimes they are just colleagues caught up in the trials and tribulations of daily struggles. In any case, Jesus insists in the next three passages that these events are not as easy to ascertain in elaborate detail as we might think. Catastrophes are just a prelude to the grandeur that will come with the Son of Man's kingdom.

> [29] "Immediately after the tribulation of those days,
>   the sun will be darkened,
>   and the moon will not give its light,
>   and the stars will fall from the sky,
>   and the powers of the heavens will be shaken.
> [30] And then the sign of the Son of Man will appear in heaven, and all the tribes of the earth will mourn, and they will see the Son of Man coming upon the clouds of heaven with power and great glory. [31] And he will send out his angels with a trumpet blast, and they will gather his elect from the four winds, from one end of the heavens to the other. [32] Learn a lesson from the fig tree. When its branch becomes tender and sprouts leaves, you know that summer is near. [33] In the same way, when you see all these things, know that he is near, at the gates. [34] Amen, I say to you, this generation will not pass away until all these things have taken place. [35] Heaven and earth will pass away, but my words will not pass away."

The very next section is filled with stock apocalyptic imagery from prophetic literature that portrays the victorious coming of the Son of Man (vv. 29-31; cf. Jl 2:1-2; Zep 1:15-16). Trumpet blasts, eclipses and other heavenly phenomena will accompany the gathering of the "elect." Jesus urges the disciples to pay attention to the signs around them, just as they would predict the coming of the seasons by the condition of the fig tree, paradoxically the symbol of peace (vv. 32-35). The immediacy of these events is emphasized by the statement that "this generation" will not pass away until these events are accomplished (cf. the negative connotation of "this generation," 11:16; 12:41-42; 23:36). Jesus even promises that his words will never pass away even if heaven and earth—that is, all reality—would pass away (v. 35). What kind of time schedule does this indicate?

[36] "But of that day and hour no one knows, neither the angels of heaven, nor the Son, but the Father alone. [37] For as it was in the days of Noah, so it will be at the coming of the Son of Man. [38] In (those) days before the flood, they were eating and drinking, marrying and giving in marriage, up to the day that Noah entered the ark. [39] They did not know until the flood came and carried them all away. So will it be (also) at the coming of the Son of Man. [40] Two men will be out in the field; one will be taken, and one will be left. [41] Two women will be grinding at the mill; one will be taken, and one will be left. [42] Therefore, stay awake! For you do not know on which day your Lord will come. [43] Be sure of this: if the master of the house had known the hour of night when the thief was coming, he would have stayed awake and not let his house be broken into. [44] So too, you also must be prepared, for at an hour you do not expect, the Son of Man will come."

At first glance we might suspect that Jesus is advising his disciples to become survivalists, to stock up now for events that are around the corner. But this interpretation mistakes urgency for a specific timetable. The next section of the discourse clarifies that the disciples are not to be absorbed by speculations about *when* these events will take place (vv. 36-44). In fact, Matthew preserves Mark's version of Jesus' saying that insists no one but God alone knows the time. "But of that day or hour, no one knows, neither the angels in heaven, nor the Son, but only the Father" (v. 36; cf. Mk 13:32). The purpose of this lengthy and detailed discourse is to make the disciples prepared (v. 44). To that end, Jesus invokes images of Israel's past, such as the time of the great flood, when people ignored the warnings about impending destruction and only Noah and his family were saved (vv. 37-39; cf. Gn 6–7). Destruction can come upon anyone at any time. Just as tornadoes sometimes hit and miss in the same neighborhood, so it will be with the coming judgment. One person will be taken, another left behind (vv. 40-41). Disciples are to be prepared for any eventuality.

The Faithful and the Unfaithful Servant (24:45-51)

⁴⁵ "Who, then, is the faithful and prudent servant, whom the master has put in charge of his household to distribute to them their food at the proper time? ⁴⁶ Blessed is that servant whom his master on his arrival finds doing so. ⁴⁷ Amen, I say to you, he will put him in charge of all his property. ⁴⁸ But if that wicked servant says to himself, 'My master is long delayed,' ⁴⁹ and begins to beat his fellow servants, and eat and drink with drunkards, ⁵⁰ the servant's master will come on an unexpected day and at an unknown hour ⁵¹ and will punish him severely and assign him a place with the hypocrites, where there will be wailing and grinding of teeth."

To conclude this first part of the discourse, Jesus uses a contrasting image of the faithful and unfaithful servant (vv. 45-51). Just as he had concluded the Sermon on the Mount with a dualistic image that emphasized the need to make a decision for discipleship (the rocky or sandy foundation; 7:24-27), so he offers the disciples a choice here. One can either be a faithful servant who manages his master's goods well or an unfaithful one who dallies while his master is away. The metaphorical dimension of the story can be seen by the use of the verb "doing so" (*poiein*), a verb used in contexts emphasizing "doing" God's will (5:19; 7:21-22,24,26; 21:31). Upon the master's sudden and unexpected return from a journey, the good servant is found prepared, while the bad servant is caught abusing the master's property and leading the "good life." The unfaithful servant will be punished severely. He is reckoned with the "hypocrites," a term that calls to mind Jesus' condemnation of the Jewish leaders in chapter 23, and he is consigned to the wailing and gnashing of teeth that accompanies final judgment (v. 51).

I suggest that these texts are not trying to frighten us into fruitless worry about our fate. Jesus is not seeking to create paranoid disciples. Rather, these teachings urge disciples to remain ever vigilant in their expectation of the parousia, the coming of the Son of Man in glory. Contrary to those who would speculate endlessly about timetables and sequences of events, the apocalyptic imagery sets the context and provides the backdrop to the unknown. Every individual, no matter his or her state in life, ultimately confronts the moment of death alone. At the very least, one can understand that in terms of this one very human reality most of us know not the day nor the hour. Jesus' words, however, go beyond the notion of death to concern the fate of our eternal lives. Matthew portrays Jesus insisting that how we live on this earth will affect how we will live in the next. The two are inextricably interrelated. "Be prepared" is not just a motto for Boy Scouts. It is a hallmark of authentic discipleship.

The Ten Virgins (25:1-13)

[1] "Then the kingdom of heaven will be like ten virgins who took their lamps and went out to meet the bridegroom. [2] Five of them were foolish and five were wise. [3] The foolish ones, when taking their lamps, brought no oil with them, [4] but the wise brought flasks of oil with their lamps. [5] Since the bridegroom was long delayed, they all became drowsy and fell asleep. [6] At midnight, there was a cry, 'Behold, the bridegroom! Come out to meet him!' [7] Then all those virgins got up and trimmed their lamps. [8] The foolish ones said to the wise, 'Give us some of your oil, for our lamps are going out.' [9] But the wise ones replied, 'No, for there may not be enough for us and you. Go instead to the merchants and buy some for yourselves.' [10] While they went off to buy it, the bridegroom came and those who were ready went into the wedding feast with him. Then the door was locked. [11] Afterwards the other virgins came and said, 'Lord, Lord, open the door for us!' [12] But he said in reply, 'Amen, I say to you, I do not know you.' [13] Therefore, stay awake, for you know neither the day nor the hour."

The next chapter reinforces and expands this apocalyptic scenario with a series of three parables (25:1-46). The first parable compares the kingdom of heaven to ten virgins (vv. 1-13). Typical of apocalyptic thought, this story offers only two choices. You are either a "wise virgin," who is prepared for the bridegroom's sudden return, or you are a "foolish virgin" who is unprepared. Matthew has also allegorized this story. The wise virgins (=industrious disciples) attend the wedding celebration (=God's kingdom) with extra oil for their lamps in case of a delay; the foolish ones (=lax disciples) have no extra oil and have to depart to buy some. Unexpectedly, the bridegroom (=Christ) who had been delayed (=delay of the parousia) comes while they are away and when the try to enter the wedding reception, the door is locked (=final judgment). Their cry echoes Jesus' warning in the Sermon on the Mount: "Not everyone who says to me, 'Lord, Lord,' will enter the kingdom of heaven . . ." (7:21; cf. 24:11-12). Crying out even the proper title of respect and faith is insufficient preparation for the kingdom; one must remain ever ready and accomplish God's will. The parable concludes with the firm exhortation to stay awake (=remain expectantly alert) because one knows not the day or hour of the master's return. It confirms Jesus' bald statement earlier that only the Father knows (24:36).

The Talents (25:14-30)

[14] "It will be as when a man who was going on a journey called in his servants and entrusted his possessions to them. [15] To one he gave five talents; to another, two; to a third, one—to each according to his ability. Then he went away. Immediately [16] the one who received five talents went and traded with them, and made another five. [17] Likewise, the one who received two made another two. [18] But the man who received one went off and dug a hole in the ground and buried his master's money. [19] After a long time the master of those servants came back and settled accounts with them. [20] The one who had received five talents came forward bringing the additional five. He said, 'Master, you gave me five talents.

See, I have made five more.' [21] His master said to him, 'Well done, my good and faithful servant. Since you were faithful in small matters, I will give you great responsibilities. Come, share your master's joy.' [22] [Then] the one who had received two talents also came forward and said, 'Master, you gave me two talents. See, I have made two more.' [23] His master said to him, 'Well done, my good and faithful servant. Since you were faithful in small matters, I will give you great responsibilities. Come, share your master's joy.' [24] Then the one who had received the one talent came forward and said, 'Master, I knew you were a demanding person, harvesting where you did not plant and gathering where you did not scatter; [25] so out of fear I went off and buried your talent in the ground. Here it is back.' [26] His master said to him in reply, 'You wicked, lazy servant! So you knew that I harvest where I did not plant and gather where I did not scatter? [27] Should you not then have put my money in the bank so that I could have got it back with interest on my return? [28] Now then! Take the talent from him and give it to the one with ten. [29] For to everyone who has, more will be given and he will grow rich; but from the one who has not, even what he has will be taken away. [30] And throw this useless servant into the darkness outside, where there will be wailing and grinding of teeth.' "

The second parable builds upon this image with a story about talents, a coin of very high value (vv. 14-30). A talent was worth about six thousand *denarii,* a *denarius* being the equivalent of a day's wage (20:2). A man goes away and entrusts varying degrees of money to three individual servants. The one with five talents invests it and makes another five. The second servant with two talents does the same. But the third servant with one talent, being more timid and fearful of his master's demanding ways, buries his talent for safekeeping. Upon the master's return, he makes each servant account for his money, rewarding the first two servants with greater responsibilities for their enterprising ways. He severely reprimands the third servant, however, for his fearful lack of enterprise. His punishment is to lose the one talent he was given and to be consigned to the outer darkness to weep and gnash his teeth.

The demanding nature of the master is clear. The gospel must be preached with fervor, and faith must be exercised with ingenuity. There is no room for timidity in God's kingdom. One must be bold. One must also utilize whatever gift he or she has been given to the fullest extent possible. Preachers have often noticed that the word "talent" connotes an innate gift. The English word comes from the Greek and Latin root for this measure of money. Each person has certain "talents" God has entrusted to him or her. This is, however, a later interpretation and one that goes beyond the type exhortation of the parable. Notice that talents are not simply inborn but God-given. How we put them to use matters. The parable concerns good stewardship in the context of potential judgment. It is a clarion call to risk something for the sake of God's kingdom. Faith is not a matter in which one can securely know one's fate. It involves a risk, a willingness to take the chance that we will make the right choices in life and obtain our reward when the master comes for an accounting. Fearfulness is one of the great obstacles to authentic faith. This parable, coming as it does so near the passion narrative in which Jesus will be betrayed, denied and deserted by those closest to him, is a warning about not being fearful even in the face of dire consequences. The message is pertinent today. Many people are fearful of many things, most especially the rapid pace of change in society. Religion, however, can become a security blanket in an irresponsible fashion. Faith means not knowing beyond the shadow of a doubt, but trusting.

The Parable of the Sheep and Goats (25:31-46)

[31] "When the Son of Man comes in his glory, and all the angels with him, he will sit upon his glorious throne, [32] and all the nations will be assembled before him. And he will separate them one from another, as a shepherd separates the

sheep from the goats. ³³ He will place the sheep on his right and the goats on his left. ³⁴ Then the king will say to those on his right, 'Come, you who are blessed by my Father. Inherit the kingdom prepared for you from the foundation of the world. ³⁵ For I was hungry and you gave me food, I was thirsty and you gave me drink, a stranger and you welcomed me, ³⁶ naked and you clothed me, ill and you cared for me, in prison and you visited me.' ³⁷ Then the righteous will answer him and say, 'Lord, when did we see you hungry and feed you, or thirsty and give you drink? ³⁸ When did we see you a stranger and welcome you, or naked and clothe you? ³⁹ When did we see you ill or in prison, and visit you?' ⁴⁰ And the king will say to them in reply, 'Amen, I say to you, whatever you did for one of these least brothers of mine, you did for me.' ⁴¹ Then he will say to those on his left, 'Depart from me, you accursed, into the eternal fire prepared for the devil and his angels. ⁴² For I was hungry and you gave me no food, I was thirsty and you gave me no drink, ⁴³ a stranger and you gave me no welcome, naked and you gave me no clothing, ill and in prison, and you did not care for me.' ⁴⁴ Then they will answer and say, 'Lord, when did we see you hungry or thirsty or a stranger or naked or ill or in prison, and not minister to your needs?' ⁴⁵ He will answer them, 'Amen, I say to you, what you did not do for one of these least ones, you did not do for me.' ⁴⁶ And these will go off to eternal punishment, but the righteous to eternal life."

The third and final parable climaxes this chapter and the entire apocalyptic discourse. It is the great parable of the sheep and goats, the day of judgment (vv. 31-46). Many treatises have been written about this magnificent story. It is unique to Matthew's Gospel and provides a suitable climax to the final discourse of Jesus. Again, OT background looms large. Sheep and goats were easily distinguished in biblical times. Sheep were considered noble animals and were respected for their silence in the face of danger (Is 53:7). Goats were considered shameful animals and often were associated with sin (cf. the "scapegoat," Lv 16:21-22).

Both creatures, of course, provided some necessities of life, such as milk, meat, wool for clothes, or goat hair for tents. The OT mentions these animals most frequently as domesticated creatures, but sometimes they were used symbolically to represent different types of individuals (Ez 34:17-24). Of all the Gospels, Matthew alone uses the imagery of sheep and goats with the greatest frequency (7:15; 9:36; 10:6,16; 12:11-12; 15:24; 18:12; 26:31), mostly in symbolic contexts.

As with many of the parables of Jesus, this one wavers somewhat in its imagery. The comparison is made between the Son of Man who will come in judgment of the nations and a shepherd who separates sheep from goats (v. 31-32). Then the image shifts to a king (v. 34) who questions the righteous and the wicked about their respective deeds (vv. 34-45). The questions of the two groups of people (literally, nations) and the responses by the king are highly repetitious, thereby strengthening the instruction. They review what have become the traditional corporal works of mercy: feeding the hungry, giving drink to the thirsty, welcoming strangers, clothing the naked, caring for the sick, and visiting the imprisoned. A real question is the meaning of the word "nations" (*ethne*). Often it denotes the Gentiles as compared to the Jews (4:15; 12:18); it can also mean "group of people" in a wider sense (21:43; 24:7). Note that the king first pronounces a judgment on each group prior to their request for an explanation about why they are either rewarded for their good deeds or punished for their omission of such deeds. In each case the king responds that whatever they did or did not do to "one of these least brothers of mine" (vv. 40,45) was unwittingly directed toward the king. The sheep (=righteous) are sent to their reward and gathered on the right side, while the goats (=unrighteous) are gathered on the left side and condemned to eternal punishment. The association of right with good and left with evil is very ancient, but it is not a universal judgment about being right- or left-handed. It may simply reflect the fact that the majority of people are right-handed.

Scholars are split on the interpretation of this particular parable. The language is ambiguous. One line of interpretation says that the "least ones" (vv. 40,45) refers to anyone in need, and that the nations assembled before the king represent any group of people. This generalizes the parable into the challenge to alleviate suffering of any kind wherever it is encountered. This view promotes Christian charity outwardly directed. Another option is to note that such language in Matthew always refers to the disciples of Jesus. In this case, the parable would be directed to the Gentiles who either treat Jesus' disciples well or ignore or abuse them. The latter interpretation obviously restricts the application of the parable to "insiders," inwardly directed toward their own treatment, whereas the former interpretation universalizes the message. Both interpretations are possible. I believe, in the context of Matthew's Gospel, the latter interpretation is the more correct. Nevertheless, the universalized interpretation is so prevalent in the tradition that it can also be respected.

Most important is to understand the spiritual teaching of the parable. As the conclusion of the great eschatological discourse, the parable draws attention to the practical, ethical application of Jesus' teaching to be loving, merciful and kind to those in need. Kindness to others honors God. We often do not know who the stranger or the fellow disciple we encounter might actually be. While the scene promises a day of reckoning, a final judgment, its purpose is less to threaten than to entice us to live out the commands of Jesus. It provides a fitting conclusion to the image of the victorious Son of Man, the coming judge, that opened the discourse under the strong influence of Daniel 7:12-14. Jesus fulfills that prophetic vision perfectly. He is the shepherd, the king, and the judge. He is the one who has consistently called his disciples to the greater righteousness and who has challenged his followers in this latter section of the Gospel to put his teaching into practice and not to be like hypocrites who profess one thing but do another.

There is no escaping this strong ethical vision. Matthew calls us to an accounting. The parable spiritually can serve a dual purpose. On the one hand, it provides a measure of comfort and incentive for the missionary efforts of the Matthean community. They should proceed to evangelize without worry about how they will be treated because "the Gentiles" will be called to account. On the other hand, everyone who would be Jesus' disciple will be measured against the standards of the ethical treatment of those in need. As Pope John Paul II has reminded us, faith and morality are indeed inextricably intertwined. While, for Matthew, only Jesus perfectly fulfills this vision, this fact does not diminish the impact this parable is to have on all of his disciples.

VI

The Passion, Death and Resurrection
(26:1–28:20)

The final section of the Gospel begins with the formula that ends the fifth discourse and that concluded each of the great discourses: "When Jesus finished all these words . . ." (26:1; cf. 7:28). The time of Jesus' teaching in word is now over. The moment of his passion is near when his identity as God's obedient and faithful Son will be most tested and vindicated. The events narrated in these final three chapters of Matthew are sequentially and chronologically ordered. They closely follow the outline of Mark's passion narrative (Mk 14–15) but with typically Matthean polish. For Matthew, Jesus' passion is not simply a story of a miscarriage of justice but of the embrace of Jesus' destiny as God's Son. His unexpected and different messiahship confirms his unique identity first pronounced in the infancy narrative (Mt 1–2) and seen throughout the story of Jesus' ministry yet ironically rejected by the ones who should have accepted him. The driving force in the Matthean passion is irony. As the familiar story of Jesus' fate unfolds, Matthew draws subtle attention to its many ironic elements.

From a spiritual standpoint, it is the image of Jesus himself that provides the focus in these final chapters. We are so familiar with the story that we have a tendency, as with the infancy narratives of Matthew and Luke, to blend the passion narratives of the four Gospels into one seamless sequence of events. Our attempt here is to focus primarily on Matthew's telling of the story. Matthew's way of describing the passion in detail, and his emphasis on the figure of Jesus throughout the ordeal, provides a prayerful portrait. As the Letter to the

Hebrews reminds us, we should keep our eyes fixed on Jesus (Heb 12:2). If you like classical music, Johann Sebastian Bach's *Matthäuspassion* ("Passion according to St. Matthew") is a sublime musical meditation on Matthew's text. It has become a staple in my own Holy Week meditations, and it complements the Gospel well.

The Beginning of the Conspiracy (26:1-5)

[1] When Jesus finished all these words, he said to his disciples, [2] "You know that in two days' time it will be Passover, and the Son of Man will be handed over to be crucified." [3] Then the chief priests and the elders of the people assembled in the palace of the high priest, who was called Caiaphas, [4] and they consulted together to arrest Jesus by treachery and put him to death. [5] But they said, "Not during the festival, that there may not be a riot among the people."

The first little scene reiterates the treachery that is about to take place. Jesus' own words set the passion story in motion. He reminds his disciples that the Passover and the foreseen time of his betrayal are near (26:2). His words are like a fourth passion prediction in shortened form. The chief priests and elders then collude with the high priest Caiaphas to put Jesus to death by treachery but not during the Jewish festival, since it could cause a disturbance among the people (26:3-5). Paradoxically, their desire to avoid the time of Passover for their dark deed is defeated as the events unfold just at that time. This shows that God is in charge, not them.

There follows a sequence of events in chapter 26 that center on the Passover and arrest of Jesus:

- Jesus is prophetically anointed in preparation for his death (vv. 6-13)

- Judas betrays Jesus to the Jewish leaders (vv. 14-16)

- the Last Supper is prepared and takes place (vv. 17-30)
- Jesus foretells Peter's denial (vv. 31-35)
- Jesus prays in the garden (vv. 36-46)
- Jesus is arrested and is brought before the Sanhedrin (vv. 47-56, 57-68)
- Peter denies Jesus (vv. 69-75).

As I have said, the focus of attention is intensely on Jesus. Matthew emphasizes this by frequently repeating Jesus' name, which reminds us of its salvific significance (1:21). His actions will fulfill his ministry to save his people from their sinfulness.

Anointing of Jesus by a Woman (26:6-13)

[6] Now when Jesus was in Bethany in the house of Simon the leper, [7] a woman came up to him with an alabaster jar of costly perfumed oil, and poured it on his head while he was reclining at table. [8] When the disciples saw this, they were indignant and said, "Why this waste? [9] It could have been sold for much, and the money given to the poor." [10] Since Jesus knew this, he said to them, "Why do you make trouble for the woman? She has done a good thing for me. [11] The poor you will always have with you; but you will not always have me. [12] In pouring this perfumed oil upon my body, she did it to prepare me for burial. [13] Amen, I say to you, wherever this gospel is proclaimed in the whole world, what she has done will be spoken of, in memory of her."

The anointing of Jesus by a nameless woman while he is at the house of an outcast, Simon the leper, reminds the readers of Jesus' continual reaching out to lowly people during his public ministry (vv. 6-13). Later Christian tradition identified this woman as Mary Magdalene, but Matthew makes no such connection. Instead she is one of a group of faithful women followers of Jesus who, in contrast to his male disciples, do not betray, deny, or flee from him in his hour of need (cf. 26:56 with 27:56,61; 28:1). Sometimes we overlook those who truly are faithful. How easy it is to gloss over the insignificant, the powerless, the disenfranchised, the poor. They become virtually invisible to us. Jesus promises that this woman's gesture will be remembered wherever the gospel is proclaimed (v. 13).

The ensuing objection by the disciples that the costly ointment used for the anointing should have been sold to provide money for the poor leads to one of the most misunderstood lines of the Gospel tradition. Jesus' reprimand about the abiding poor is neither a put-down nor an ignoring of those who are poor. Rather, this prophetic anointing which simultaneously confirms Jesus' messianic and royal lineage and prepares him for burial is a rare, profound gesture of love most appropriate to its context. In this instance, allowing her to anoint him, even with costly oil, is part of the divine drama being acted out. While the bridegroom is present, he must be honored (9:15). One will not always have this opportunity to honor the messiah, but sadly the poor remain a reality in every era (see Dt 15:11). This is not a call to let the poor remain poor. Instead, the woman's gesture paradoxically shows that some of life's lowly ones can perceive the greater good when they encounter it.

The Betrayal (26:14-16)

[14] Then one of the Twelve, who was called Judas Iscariot, went to the chief priests [15] and said, "What are you willing to give me if I hand him over to you?" They paid him thirty pieces of silver, [16] and from that time on he looked for an opportunity to hand him over.

The anonymous prophetic anointing by an outsider contrasts greatly with the next scene of the betrayal by an insider (vv. 14-16). Judas, with the epitaph of his deed attached to him throughout the Gospel (10:4), freely offers to hand Jesus over for the paltry price paid for a slave (Ex 21:32) or payment to a substitute shepherd (Zec 11:12), an allusion to OT texts. In fact, this OT background recalls that Judas' action, despicable though it be, is actually fulfilling God's Word (Zec 11:11; cf. Mt 27:3-10). God is indeed in charge. Judas reminds us that being an insider, being chosen by Jesus himself, does not necessarily ensure our fidelity. One must work at faithfulness.

The Last Supper (26:17-35)

[17] On the first day of the Feast of Unleavened Bread, the disciples approached Jesus and said, "Where do you want us to prepare for you to eat the Passover?" [18] He said, "Go into the city to a certain man and tell him, 'The teacher says, "My appointed time draws near; in your house I shall celebrate the Passover with my disciples." ' " [19] The disciples then did as Jesus had ordered, and prepared the Passover.

[20] When it was evening, he reclined at table with the Twelve. [21] And while they were eating, he said, "Amen, I say to you, one of you will betray me." [22] Deeply distressed at this, they began to say to him one after another, "Surely it is not I, Lord?" [23] He said in reply, "He who has dipped his hand into the dish with me is the one who will betray me. [24] The Son of Man indeed goes, as it is written of him, but woe to that man by whom the Son of Man is betrayed. It would be better for that man if he had never been born." [25] Then Judas, his betrayer, said in reply, "Surely it is not I, Rabbi?" He answered, "You have said so."

[26] While they were eating, Jesus took bread, said the blessing, broke it, and giving it to his disciples said, "Take and eat; this is my body." [27] Then he took a cup, gave thanks, and gave it to them, saying, "Drink from it, all of you, [28] for this is my blood of the covenant, which will be shed on behalf of many for the forgiveness of sins. [29] I tell you, from now on I shall not drink this fruit of the vine until the day when I drink it with you new in the kingdom of my Father." [30] Then, after singing a hymn, they went out to the Mount of Olives.

The next scene describes the Last Supper which took place around the time of the holiest Jewish feast of Passover, combined (as it was in Jesus' day) with the feast of Unleavened Bread (vv. 17-30). Jesus directs the Passover preparations of his disciples with the reminder that "my appointed time draws near" (v. 18). The appointed time (*kairos*) often refers to the end time, the time of the harvest or the vintage (see 8:29; 13:30; 21:34). Here it prophetically refers to Jesus' own hour of passion, death and resurrection. The timing of the Last Supper, at least in Matthew's view, heightens the significance of Jesus' death. The Passover commemorated God's most loving action on behalf of the chosen people, the exodus event (Ex 12–14). In Jesus God now acts even more definitively to liberate God's people.

Jesus' action will be the ransom of many for it will save people from their sins (26:28; cf. 20:28). But the first action while at table with his disciples is to announce the betrayal. Jesus' sudden revelation leads to a soul-searching denial on the part of the disciples. Judas likewise joins the denial with the question, "Surely it is not I, Rabbi?" (v. 25). Jesus' simple response. "You have said so," returns the blame to Judas' own lips. He also prophetically notes that it would be better for such a man not to have been born, words that foreshadow Judas' suicide (26:24; cf. 27:3-10). Betrayal is probably one of the worst offenses against love and friendship. It violates the deepest trust that human beings can know. Little wonder that traitors are often despised by those who use them for their own ends, as well as by those who experience the betrayal. Judas is a pathetic figure in Matthew, but we should also not forget that he was a vehicle for fulfilling God's will. Paradoxically, his despicable action coincides with God's intentions, and the result is salvation.

At the supper itself Matthew describes the eucharistic actions that bespeak the liturgy of the Church (26:26-30). Jesus took, blessed, broke, and gave the bread to his disciples (cf. 14:19; 15:36), identifying himself with the bread of the exodus. Then he took the cup of wine, identified as his blood, and shared it with them as a sign of the forgiveness of sins. Even at the time of betrayal Jesus can do no other than to continue his saving work. He also foresees that he will not "drink" this cup again until he drinks it with them in the kingdom of his Father. The entire picture is painted in hues that reflect the Jewish Passover ritual. The blessings, the prayers of thanksgiving, the blessing of the cup of wine, and the concluding hymn as they depart to the Mount of Olives all point to a ritual meal. Scholars debate whether or not the Last Supper was historically a Passover meal. Matthew, however, portrays it in this fashion and makes of it a powerful eucharistic action that likely reflects the liturgical practice of his community. Judas' betrayal is balanced by Jesus' willing sacrifice of himself.

[31] Then Jesus said to them, "This night all of you will have your faith in me shaken, for it is written:
    'I will strike the shepherd,
    and the sheep of the flock will be dispersed';
[32] but after I have been raised up, I shall go before you to Galilee." [33] Peter said to him in reply, "Though all may have their faith in you shaken, mine will never be." [34] Jesus said to him, "Amen, I say to you, this very night before the cock crows, you will deny me three times." [35] Peter said to him, "Even though I should have to die with you, I will not deny you." And all the disciples spoke likewise.

Continuing the motif of Jesus prophetically informing his disciples of the events about to unfold, he predicts that their faith in him will be shaken (vv. 31-35). Their "little faith" is not sufficient to withstand the challenge to come. Jesus and his disciples proceed from the Supper to the Mount of Olives. Jesus quotes the OT to make the point that once the shepherd is struck down, the sheep will scatter (Zec 13:7). The warning is accompanied by a hopeful promise: after the resurrection he will precede them to Galilee. Peter, again in the role of spokesman for the rest, responds with bravado: "Though all may have their faith in you shaken, mine will never be" (v. 33).

One need only recall the other scenes in the Gospel in which Peter puts up a brave front, only to fall flat (14:28-31; 16:16,22-23; 19:27). This leads to Jesus' forecast that before the cock crows that night Peter will deny Jesus not once, but three times. Peter's response to that is evidence that he is actually in denial! He does not fathom his own inner weakness. The disciples all protest that this will not occur. Peter, at this point, becomes a reminder that, paraphrased, says: "the bigger they are, the harder they fall." Peter's rock solid faith is not on as firm a foundation as he bravely asserts. Perhaps it is over-security, perhaps it is simply naivete. Neither his hollow rhetoric nor his position protects him from failing the ultimate test. He provides fair warning to all who would rely on their own ability rather than on the Lord's strength.

Agony in the Garden (26:36-56)

[36] Then Jesus came with them to a place called Gethsemane, and he said to his disciples, "Sit here while I go over there and pray." [37] He took along Peter and the two sons of Zebedee, and began to feel sorrow and distress. [38] Then he said to them, "My soul is sorrowful even to death. Remain here and keep watch with me." [39] He advanced a little and fell prostrate in prayer, saying, "My Father, if it is possible, let this cup pass from me; yet, not as I will, but as you will." [40] When he returned to his disciples he found them asleep. He said to Peter, "So you could not keep watch with me for one hour? [41] Watch and pray that you may not undergo the test. The spirit is willing, but the flesh is weak." [42] Withdrawing a second time, he prayed again, "My Father, if it is not possible that this cup pass without my drinking it, your will be done!" [43] Then he returned once more and found them asleep, for they could not keep their eyes open. [44] He left them and withdrew again and prayed a third time, saying the same thing again. [45] Then he returned to his disciples and said to them, "Are you still sleeping and taking your rest? Behold, the hour

is at hand when the Son of Man is to be handed over to sinners. [46] Get up, let us go. Look, my betrayer is at hand."

The next scene takes place in Gethsemane. It portrays a time of prayer in the garden (vv. 36-46). Traditionally called the "agony in the garden," in Matthew it is more of a scene of intense prayer on the part of Jesus to wrestle with his fate. Unlike Luke's account, the word "agony" does not appear (Lk 22:39-46; *agonia* refers to intense preparations for an athletic contest). Instead we see Jesus' withdrawal with his inner circle of Peter and the two sons of Zebedee to a quiet place in the garden where he can pour out his soul to his heavenly Father. He asks of his companions that they remain and "keep watch with" him. Watchfulness was a key element of Jesus' apocalyptic teaching, a sign of faithful discipleship (24:42; 25:13). Being *with* Jesus in his time of trial paradoxically recalls that he is Emmanuel, God *with* us (26:38,40; cf. 1:23; 18:20; 28:20). The disciples, however, are not up to the task. They fall asleep.

Three times Jesus prays that the cup (=his suffering and death) would pass from him, and three times he finds that they are unable to keep vigil. Jesus' prayer is indeed part of the same prayer he had taught his disciples in the Sermon on the Mount: "your will be done" (v. 42; cf. 6:10). What is essential is not avoiding his fate but embracing it because it is the will of his Father (*thelema*; cf. 7:21; 12:50; 21:31). In the end, he excuses the failure of the disciples to keep watch because of human frailty rather than ill will, and he goes to meet his betrayer because his "hour" has arrived. This poignant scene in Matthew has a special reverence. The intensity of Jesus' prayer, the exhortation to his friends to keep vigil, the honesty of the request to his Father, and the ultimate surrender to God's will are powerful gestures. If Jesus undergoes such testing in a time of trial, how can we expect to avoid it? Yet the vital issue is surrender to God's will. For us God's will might not be quite so transparent as Matthew indicates here, nor are our friends necessarily so blatant in their inability to stay vigilant, but we should not be surprised to find ourselves in a circumstance of drinking from a cup we would rather avoid. In such moments, prayer becomes essential. The simple words, "your will be done," can become almost a mantra, a repeated formula to remind ourselves, nay, to convince ourselves that faith demands this final surrender. Jesus himself was not without this moment of trial, but neither was it the final temptation, as we shall see.

Arrest and Desertion (26:47-56)

[47] While he was still speaking, Judas, one of the Twelve, arrived, accompanied by a large crowd, with swords and clubs, who had come from the chief priests and the elders of the people. [48] His betrayer had arranged a sign with them, saying, "The man I shall kiss is the one; arrest him." [49] Immediately he went over to Jesus and said, "Hail, Rabbi!" and he kissed him. [50] Jesus answered him, "Friend, do what you have come for." Then stepping forward they laid hands on Jesus and arrested him. [51] And behold, one of those who accompanied Jesus put his hand to his sword, drew it, and struck the high priest's servant, cutting off his ear. [52] Then Jesus said to him, "Put your sword back into its sheath, for all who take the sword will perish by the sword.

[53] "Do you think that I cannot call upon my Father and he will not provide me at this moment with more than twelve legions of angels? [54] But then how would the scriptures be fulfilled which say that it must come to pass in this way?" [55] At that hour Jesus said to the crowds, "Have you come out as against a robber, with swords and clubs to seize me? Day after day I sat teaching in the temple area, yet you did not arrest me. [56] But all this has come to pass that the writings of the prophets may be fulfilled." Then all the disciples left him and fled.

Again Jesus' words carry the action forward. Jesus issues the command to meet the betrayer (v. 46), and thus sets into

190

motion the next several scenes of arrest, trial, and mockery (vv. 47-68). The crowd and Jewish authorities arrive fully armed as if they seek a brigand. Judas' prearranged signal of an ironic "kiss," a friendly gesture gone awry, instigates the arrest. Jesus even addresses him with the ironic title, "friend." For one brief moment one of Jesus' companions—he is not named—attempts to show bravery by striking out with a sword and cutting off the ear of a servant. Jesus' response is abrupt. He commands that the sword be sheathed and explains that this is his Father's will. One does not repay violence with violence (5:38-39). If he wanted to, he could easily call out to his Father who would provide legions of angels to assist him (remember the ministering angels at the temptation, 4:11), "but then how would the scriptures be fulfilled . . .?" (v. 54) For Matthew, the scriptures are of paramount importance. He goes on to state that the prophetic writings are dictating the entire event, an indication that God is in charge (v. 56). This is not the same thing as saying that Jesus is going through a charade. On the contrary, Jesus experienced true temptation and true suffering. Matthew is simply reminding us that the dynamic of prophecy and fulfillment, so functional in Jesus' story, is the way God's will is accomplished. The prophetic word comes to pass because it is authentic and true.

The Trial and Judgment (26:57–27:2)

[57] Those who had arrested Jesus led him away to Caiaphas the high priest, where the scribes and the elders were assembled. [58] Peter was following him at a distance as far as the high priest's courtyard, and going inside he sat down with the servants to see the outcome. [59] The chief priests and the entire Sanhedrin kept trying to obtain false testimony against Jesus in order to put him to death, [60] but they found none, though many false witnesses came forward. Finally two came forward [61] who stated, "This man said, 'I can destroy the temple of God and within three days rebuild it.'" [62] The high priest rose

and addressed him, "Have you no answer? What are these men testifying against you?" [63] But Jesus was silent. Then the high priest said to him, "I order you to tell us under oath before the living God whether you are the Messiah, the Son of God." [64] Jesus said to him in reply, "You have said so. But I tell you:

From now on
you will see 'the Son of Man
seated at the right hand of the Power'
and 'coming on the clouds of heaven.'"

[65] Then the high priest tore his robes and said, "He has blasphemed! What further need have we of witnesses? You have now heard the blasphemy; [66] what is your opinion?" They said in reply, "He deserves to die!" [67] Then they spat in his face and struck him, while some slapped him, [68] saying, "Prophesy for us, Messiah: who is it that struck you?"

The crowd then leads Jesus before the high priest and the Sanhedrin (vv. 57-68). Scholars have long debated the legalities of such a scene. There are many legal questions to explore. Could the Sanhedrin hold a night hearing? Did they have the right to inflict capital punishment? Would they have mocked Jesus as the text indicates? For Matthew, such questions are not essential. He portrays the scene as a hearing before Jewish authorities who had been plotting against Jesus for a long time. This is the culmination of their jealousy, hatred, and opposition to Jesus. All they can do is attempt to assemble false testimony (v. 59), eventually succeeding with some false witnesses who testify to Jesus' preaching against the Temple (vv. 60-62). Like a sheep before its slayers, Jesus remains silent (v. 61). Only when the high priest cajoles him into admitting whether he is the Messiah, the Son of God (similar to Peter's confession, 16:16), does Jesus respond with the non-committal, "You have said so" (v. 64), the same words used of Judas' betrayal and Pilate's question (26:5; 27:11). This places the affirmation ironically on the high priest's own lips.

Jesus then adds a mysterious saying about the coming Son of Man, reminiscent of his eschatological discourse and of the expectation in the Book of Daniel (Mt 24:29-31). For reasons that are not altogether clear, this leads to the conclusion by the high priest and the assembly that Jesus has committed blasphemy. Blasphemy requires pronouncing God's name, yet Jesus' use of the paraphrastic expression "the Power" does not seem to meet that criterion. Nevertheless, he is said to deserve death, and they mock him with beatings and sarcastic cries of "Prophesy for us, Messiah. . . ." Their mockery is ironic at its core, for they do not realize that Jesus has been prophesying his fate all along and that God's prophetic writings in the OT have been guiding the affair. Of some concern is that Matthew shows the Jewish assembly doing the actual mockery of Jesus rather than mere soldiers or underlings (v. 67, "they"; cf. Mk 14:65, "some" and "guards" and Lk 22:71 and 23:11, the transposition of the mockery to Herod). Is Matthew thereby heightening anti-Jewish sentiment? If so, the reason is the same that we have stressed elsewhere in Matthew. The strong resentment toward his Jewish neighbors is related more to the intra-Jewish debates than to Christian-Jewish relations.

Denial (26:69-75)

[69] Now Peter was sitting outside in the courtyard. One of the maids came over to him and said, "You too were with Jesus the Galilean." [70] But he denied it in front of everyone, saying, "I do not know what you are talking about!" [71] As he went out to the gate, another girl saw him and said to those who were there, "This man was with Jesus the Nazorean." [72] Again he denied it with an oath, "I do not know the man!" [73] A little later the bystanders came over and said to Peter, "Surely you too are one of them; even your speech gives you away." [74] At that he began to curse and to swear, "I do not know the man." And immediately a cock crowed. [75] Then Peter remembered the word that Jesus had spoken: "Before

the cock crows you will deny me three times." He went out and began to weep bitterly.

The final scene of the chapter recounts Peter's denial (vv. 69-75). Continuing with the favored technique of three elements, Matthew narrates in escalating fashion the denial of Peter. Whereas Jesus willingly stepped forward to embrace his fate, Peter tries to retreat in the face of danger. The denials become increasingly public and intense. The first to accuse Peter of being "with Jesus the Galilean" is a maid; he denies knowing what she is talking about. Then another girl accuses him of being with "Jesus the Nazorean"; he denies with an oath that he does not know him (contrary to Jesus' prohibition of oaths, 5:34). Finally, some bystanders accuse him because his Galilean accent betrays him, and Peter curses and swears, "I do not know the man." Only then does the cock crow and remind Peter of Jesus' prophecy, at which Peter leaves the scene "to weep bitterly."

Is there really much difference between denial and betrayal? On the level of human trust, Peter's threefold denial seems almost as despicable as Judas' betrayal. Not only does he try to save his own skin by avoiding guilt by association, but he even denies that he knows Jesus. This disciple who so often spoke boldly and on behalf of others now speaks solely to defend himself, relying on curses and oaths to prop up his inability to uphold the truth. Only his response in light of his failure leads one to suspect that his regret at his cowardly action changes him later. His bitter tears must be a sign of repentance. Nowhere does Matthew recount that Peter repented his deed and was reconciled, yet his inclusion among "the eleven" in Galilee (28:16) and his later prominent role in Christian history (and in Matthew's Gospel) indicates that he, in contrast to Judas, did not despair. Perhaps Peter was able to apply Jesus' lesson of the need for forgiveness to himself (18:21-22). If we are not told *how* he came to be able to live with himself and to go on being a disciple, we can nonetheless see in him a model to observe. One

194

side of the model warns us that even the unthinkable, denial by an intimate friend, is possible. Everyone has the capability of denial. The other side reminds us that all is not lost if our fear and human frailty fail us when courage is demanded. In this fashion, Matthew paints Peter in believable, complex, and fully human hues rather than making him some idealized caricature of a super-disciple.

^{27:1} When it was morning, all the chief priests and the elders of the people took counsel against Jesus to put him to death. ² They bound him, led him away, and handed him over to Pilate, the governor.

The next chapter continues the passion with a shift of scene. The Jewish elders take counsel to put Jesus to death and hand him over to the secular authority to see the deed done (27:1-2), fulfilling Jesus' prophecy of being handed over to Gentiles (20:18-19). The use of the verb "handed over" (v. 2, *paradidomi*) recalls the treachery of Judas and unites the entire sequence of events from betrayal, to Jewish opposition, to the condemnation by Pilate (4:12; 17:22; 20:18-19; 26:15-16,45; 27:4,26). All are part of the sinful plot against Jesus (26:45, "handed over to sinners"). The reference to Pilate the governor (v. 2) recalls the warning Jesus had issued to the disciples that they, too, would be hauled before governors and kings (10:18). The servants will be treated no better than the master (10:25-26). Ironically, the "governor" will show his inability to govern as he caves into surrounding pressures that he knows to be dishonest.

The Fate of Judas (27:3-10)

³ Then Judas, his betrayer, seeing that Jesus had been condemned, deeply regretted what he had done. He returned the thirty pieces of silver to the chief priests and elders, ⁴ saying, "I have sinned in betraying innocent blood." They said, "What is that to us? Look to it yourself." ⁵ Flinging the money into the temple, he departed and went off and hanged

himself. [6] The chief priests gathered up the money, but said, "It is not lawful to deposit this in the temple treasury, for it is the price of blood." [7] After consultation, they used it to buy the potter's field as a burial place for foreigners. [8] That is why that field even today is called the Field of Blood. [9] Then was fulfilled what had been said through Jeremiah the prophet, "And they took the thirty pieces of silver, the value of a man with a price on his head, a price set by some of the Israelites, [10] and they paid it out for the potter's field just as the Lord had commanded me."

The next passage, unique to Matthew, narrates the fate of the betrayer (vv. 3-10). In contrast to Peter, Judas commits suicide by hanging (cf. the very different version of Judas' fate in Acts 2:16-19). Note that Judas, in that magic moment of 20-20 hindsight, regrets his action (v. 3, "he deeply regretted what he had done"). He even admits that he has sinned by betraying innocent blood (v. 4). The story, however, is a tale of everyone trying to distance themselves from guilt. Judas tries to return the betrayal money only to be refused by the chief priests. Then he flings the money into the Temple, but even then the Jewish leaders refuse to accept this "blood money" back into the treasury. Instead they buy a field to be used as a cemetery for strangers. Jesus' death ironically provides a final resting place for strangers.

The key to the passage is not simply found in the fate of Judas who despairs of any alternative but suicide. Matthew transforms the story into a paradoxical statement about Jesus' fate. In keeping with the flow of the passion story, Matthew focuses our attention on Jesus. It becomes a christological moment. Three times the image of blood comes to the fore (vv. 4,6,8) and the image of "innocent blood" harks back to the fate of Jeremiah the prophet who was wrongly persecuted for his prophetic words, especially for his attacks on the Temple (Jer 26:15). Matthew adds another of his telltale fulfillment citations which he attributes to Jeremiah, though it comes from a combination of OT sources (Zec 11:12-13; Jer 18–19). The more essential point is that Judas has betrayed innocent blood, a judgment that will be confirmed also by Pilate (27:24) and his wife (27:19). Jesus' innocence is what comes to the fore. His fate, like OT prophets of old, is a miscarriage of human justice even as it fulfills the divine will. It makes Jesus' refusal to defend himself and his surrender to the cross all that more poignant. On the human level, Jesus' fate because of his utter innocence is a terrible mistake. In God's eyes, however, his death is an act of loving surrender and paradoxically provides salvation for all people. Matthew reminds us once more that his story is about God's perspective and not our own (16:23).

Jesus before Pontius Pilate (27:11-31)

[11] Now Jesus stood before the governor, and he questioned him, "Are you the king of the Jews?" Jesus said, "You say so." [12] And when he was accused by the chief priests and elders, he made no answer. [13] Then Pilate said to him, "Do you not hear how many things they are testifying against you?" [14] But he did not answer him one word, so that the governor was greatly amazed.

[15] Now on the occasion of the feast the governor was accustomed to release to the crowd one prisoner whom they wished. [16] And at that time they had a notorious prisoner called [Jesus] Barabbas. [17] So when they had assembled, Pilate said to them, "Which one do you want me to release to you, [Jesus] Barabbas, or Jesus called Messiah?" [18] For he knew that it was out of envy that they had handed him over.

[19] While he was still seated on the bench, his wife sent him a message, "Have nothing to do with that righteous man. I suffered much in a dream today because of him."

[20] The chief priests and the elders persuaded the crowds to ask for Barabbas but to destroy Jesus. [21] The governor said to them in reply, "Which of the two do you want me to release to you?" They answered, "Barabbas!" [22] Pilate said to them, "Then what shall I do with Jesus called Messiah?" They all

said, "Let him be crucified!" [23] But he said, "Why? What evil has he done?" They only shouted the louder, "Let him be crucified!" [24] When Pilate saw that he was not succeeding at all, but that a riot was breaking out instead, he took water and washed his hands in the sight of the crowd, saying, "I am innocent of this man's blood. Look to it yourselves." [25] And the whole people said in reply, "His blood be upon us and upon our children." [26] Then he released Barabbas to them, but after he had Jesus scourged, he handed him over to be crucified.

[27] Then the soldiers of the governor took Jesus inside the praetorium and gathered the whole cohort around him. [28] They stripped off his clothes and threw a scarlet military cloak about him. [29] Weaving a crown out of thorns, they placed it on his head, and a reed in his right hand. And kneeling before him, they mocked him, saying, "Hail, King of the Jews!" [30] They spat upon him and took the reed and kept striking him on the head. [31] And when they had mocked him, they stripped him of the cloak, dressed him in his own clothes, and led him off to crucify him.

Then Jesus is led before the governor, questioned by him, and finally convicted and tortured (vv. 11-31). Ironically, Jesus stands in the presence of this lesser power while Pilate apparently remains seated, the normal position of authority. Pilate's question whether Jesus is the "king of the Jews" or not, and Jesus' non-committal "You say so," indicates the primary charge against him, at least from the secular perspective. Just as Herod had feared another "king" at the beginning of Matthew's story of Jesus (2:1-3), so the Roman representative of the emperor now queries whether he has a rival authority on his hands. Recently, archaeology has confirmed that "king of the Jews" may well have been a title used of Herod the Great. This fact lends historical significance to the charge against Jesus. But Matthew is less interested in history than in theology. The lengthy scene before Pilate gives Matthew another chance to emphasize in various ways that Jesus is not guilty of any of the charges against him. He is not an insurrectionist, and ironically Pilate's attempt to release him will lead instead to the release of a notorious troublemaker, Barabbas (v. 16). To make the irony even clearer, some manuscripts of Matthew show that Barabbas' (=son of the father) first name may have been Jesus. If that were the case, one Jesus son-of-the-father would be released and the other Jesus Son-of-the-Father and Messiah condemned.

Throughout the story, Matthew paints Pilate in rather positive terms. He tries to give Jesus a chance to defend himself (v. 13); he recognizes the evil intentions of the Jewish leaders (v. 18); his wife has a dream and warns her husband to have nothing to do with "that righteous man" (v. 19); he tries to release him instead of Barabbas (vv. 21-23); and he invokes his own innocence, thereby drawing attention to the "innocent blood" that he is reluctantly shedding (v. 24). Some scholars suggest that Matthew purposely downplays Pilate's role in Jesus' death and concomitantly increases the role of the Jewish leaders. There is some truth to this, but we should not forget that ultimately Pilate condemns him to scourging and crucifixion, a Roman form of death. Yet only Matthew has the ominous line spoken by "the whole people" (no longer the vacillating "crowds" seen throughout the Gospel): "His blood be upon us and upon our children" (27:25). This is one of those lines from scripture one wishes had never been written because it has led to so much misunderstanding through history. Some have falsely thought of it as a curse for all time against the Jews as a people for killing Jesus. Rather, it is an acceptance of the responsibility on that small group of people and the next generation who opposed Jesus and sought his death. For Matthew, the words are ironic. The once vacillating crowd now coalesces into a unified "whole people." They have apparently been persuaded by the scribes, chief priests, and elders *of the people.* Jesus came to save his "people" from their sins and by his blood he accomplishes that salvation (1:21; 26:28). The entire scene before Pilate, then, is focused christologically on Jesus and emphasizes his innocence.

The next part of the sequence passage is preparatory to the crucifixion, the mockery by the Roman soldiers (vv. 27-31). Just as the Jewish hearing had ended with a mockery, so does the Roman trial. The scene is artfully constructed in chiastic fashion:

Jesus is led to the praetorium
   Jesus is stripped and clothed in mock royal garb
      Jesus is crowned with thorns and given a reed scepter
         The soldiers kneel and mock him as "King of the Jews"
      Jesus is spat upon and struck on the head with the reed
   Jesus is stripped and re-clothed in his own garb
Jesus is led out to crucifixion

The whole cohort of soldiers (a huge number) mock Jesus as a "king" by dressing him up in a scarlet military cloak (a realistic touch, since military robes were red) honoring him with sarcastic rituals. The centerpiece is the gesture of mock homage and being hailed as a king. Matthew avoids using the true word for "worship" (*proskyneo*) in this passage, for it is obviously a charade. The passage ironically presents Jesus as the humble king he is (recall 21:5 and Herod's fear, 2:1-3). It provides a poignant end to the Roman scene and directly leads to the crucifixion.

The Way of the Cross and the Crucifixion (27:32-44)

> [32] As they were going out, they met a Cyrenian named Simon; this man they pressed into service to carry his cross. [33] And when they came to a place called Golgotha (which means Place of the Skull), [34] they gave Jesus wine to drink mixed with gall. But when he had tasted it, he refused to drink.

³⁵ After they had crucified him, they divided his garments by casting lots; ³⁶then they sat down and kept watch over him there. ³⁷ And they placed over his head the written charge against him: This is Jesus, the King of the Jews. ³⁸Two revolutionaries were crucified with him, one on his right and the other on his left. ³⁹ Those passing by reviled him, shaking their heads ⁴⁰and saying, "You who would destroy the temple and rebuild it in three days, save yourself, if you are the Son of God, [and] come down from the cross!" ⁴¹ Likewise the chief priests with the scribes and elders mocked him and said, ⁴²"He saved others; he cannot save himself. So he is the king of Israel! Let him come down from the cross now, and we will believe in him. ⁴³He trusted in God; let him deliver him now if he wants him. For he said, 'I am the Son of God.'" ⁴⁴The revolutionaries who were crucified with him also kept abusing him in the same way.

The way of the cross is described in one short verse in which an otherwise unknown character, Simon of Cyrene, is forced to help Jesus carry the cross (v. 32). Whether Simon is a diaspora Jew or a foreigner (perhaps representing Gentiles) is uncertain, but he is one of a cast of smaller characters who, in contrast to the inner circle of disciples, assists Jesus. Matthew proceeds immediately to the lengthy crucifixion scene (vv. 32-56). Here Jesus' identity as God's Son returns as a main theme, tied to the type of kingship which is his by virtue of his identity. The scene is also punctuated with allusions to OT passages, mostly laments from the Psalms, that reinforce the notion that all of this is happening by virtue of God's holy Word. There are two main parts to the crucifixion. The first is a mockery and temptation scene (vv. 39-44), and the second is the death (vv. 45-56).

Arriving at an ominous place called Golgotha (the Place of the Skull), a standard locale for executions outside the city (cf. 21:39), they (presumably the soldiers) try to give Jesus a narcotic drink to deaden the pain, but he refuses (v. 34; cf. Ps 69:21). Then they crucify him with two common bandits (NAB "revolutionaries"), one on his left and one on his right. These positions ironically recall the naive request of the mother of John and James, the sons of Zebeedee (cf. 20:21). They also divide his clothes by casting lots (Ps 22:18), and sit down to wait the outcome. The charge they place overhead paradoxically confirms his identity as king of the Jews and recalls the trial before Pilate and the mockery. It is a king they crucify, but not the kind they expect.

Then begins a mockery scene that might well be considered "the last temptation of Christ." Just as there were three temptations at the beginning of his ministry (4:1-11), so now there are three temptations at the most critical juncture of his ministry. Three sets of passers-by revile him and challenge Jesus in words that recall the original three temptations. At stake is his identity as the Son of God (vv. 40,43; cf. 4:3,6). If Satan conducted the first set of temptations, the last set is done by those who reflect the same mentality. God's Son, if he were truly that, should prove it by using his power miraculously on his own behalf. They ironically remember that he "saved" others; now why can he not save himself? (v. 42) To do so, of course, would violate Jesus' identity and the principles he had taught his disciples. His power is not for its own sake but for the sake of those in need. Sacrificing one's own life is the way to save others (10:39). Jesus could call on his Father to save him, but to do so would negate his Sonship (26:53). Jesus defeated the earlier temptations by relying on a profound understanding of God's Word. Now he defeats these temptations by surrender to the inevitable sacrifice he must make.

The Death of Jesus (27:45-56)

[45] From noon onward, darkness came over the whole land until three in the afternoon. [46] And about three o'clock Jesus cried out in a loud voice, "Eli, Eli, lema sabachthani?" which means, "My God, my God, why have you forsaken me?" [47] Some of the bystanders who heard it said, "This one is calling for Elijah." [48] Immediately one of them ran to get a

sponge; he soaked it in wine, and putting it on a reed, gave it to him to drink. [49] But the rest said, "Wait, let us see if Elijah comes to save him." [50] But Jesus cried out again in a loud voice, and gave up his spirit. [51] And behold, the veil of the sanctuary was torn in two from top to bottom. The earth quaked, rocks were split, [52] tombs were opened, and the bodies of many saints who had fallen asleep were raised. [53] And coming forth from their tombs after his resurrection, they entered the holy city and appeared to many. [54] The centurion and the men with him who were keeping watch over Jesus feared greatly when they saw the earthquake and all that was happening, and they said, "Truly, this was the Son of God!" [55] There were many women there, looking on from a distance, who had followed Jesus from Galilee, ministering to him. [56] Among them were Mary Magdalene and Mary the mother of James and Joseph, and the mother of the sons of Zebedee.

The second part of the passage narrates the events at the death of Jesus (vv. 45-56). Matthew does not flinch from the suffering that accompanies crucifixion. Darkness covers the earth for the final three hours of agony on the cross. It is a darkness that shrouds the dark deed. Jesus cries out in a loud voice with words of lament that recall the psalmist's complaint about being abandoned by God (v. 46; Ps 22:1). Jesus is not playing a charade. His suffering and death are real. So is his prayer to his Father ("My God"). He feels abandoned yet maintans his relationship to God and refuses to abandon his Father. He joins himself to our experience of human suffering by means of a most cruel capital punishment. His prayer is not a lack of faith but an expression of the profound depth of pain that people can sometimes experience. In the biblical mentality of lament, it is acceptable to pour out one's heart to God and cry out in anguish. We have lost something of this art. We complain and gripe, but lament is more profound. It simultaneously acknowledges human anguish while maintaining trust in God (see Ps 22:1-32).

The bystanders misunderstand Jesus' words, thinking he is calling Elijah to rescue him. But Elijah has already come in the person of John the Baptist, and his fate was similar (17:11-13). No one will come to "save" Jesus (v. 49), for his very actions are now saving all humankind, including those seated in the darkness now awaiting the outcome (cf. 4:16). At last, Jesus cries out again and freely surrenders his spirit. At that moment a series of phenomena occurs that confirms God's role in this event (vv. 51-53):

- the sanctuary curtain in the Temple is torn in two from top to bottom
- the earth is shaken (an earthquake)
- rocks are split
- tombs are opened
- many dead saints are raised and, after the resurrection, appear in the holy city.

The succession of passive verbs (in the original Greek) emphasizes that God is the power behind these actions. Just as Jesus' birth was accompanied by heavenly phenomena, so is his death. These apocalyptic phenomena herald the beginnings of a new era in the fulfillment of Israel's eschatological hope. Most striking is the rising of the saints and their witness in Jerusalem. Even at the death scene Matthew emphasizes the new life that comes out of Jesus' action. These are the holy ones of Israel who go forth to the holy city to give testimony (see Ez 37:12-13). These Jewish saints provide one form of witness; a group of Gentiles will provide another. In the face of these marvelous events, the centurion and his companions testify that "Truly, this was the Son of God!" (v. 54) Their confession of the true identity of Jesus is ironic and reflects the fact that many in Matthew's Church were, in fact, Gentile. Matthew also describes other witnesses to the events, the women who had followed Jesus from Galilee and assisted him in ministry, among whom some are named. Their presence heightens all the more the absence of the male disciples who had fled rather than risk a fate similar to Jesus (26:56).

The Burial of Jesus (27:57-66)

[57] When it was evening, there came a rich man from Arimathea named Joseph, who was himself a disciple of Jesus. [58] He went to Pilate and asked for the body of Jesus; then Pilate ordered it to be handed over. [59]Taking the body, Joseph wrapped it (in) clean linen [60] and laid it in his new tomb that he had hewn in the rock. Then he rolled a huge stone across the entrance to the tomb and departed. [61] But Mary Magdalene and the other Mary remained sitting there, facing the tomb.

[62] The next day, the one following the day of preparation, the chief priests and the Pharisees gathered before Pilate [63] and said, "Sir, we remember that this impostor while still alive said, 'After three days I will be raised up.' [64]Give orders, then, that the grave be secured until the third day, lest his disciples come and steal him and say to the people, 'He has been raised from the dead.' This last imposture would be worse than the first." [65] Pilate said to them, "The guard is yours; go secure it as best you can." [66] So they went and secured the tomb by fixing a seal to the stone and setting the guard.

The final scene of the chapter is the burial and posting of the guard (vv. 57-66). A man named Joseph had assisted Jesus at the beginning (Mt 1–2); now a different man named Joseph assists at the end. Matthew calls Joseph of Arimathea a disciple of Jesus, someone willing to take a risk. He asks Pilate directly for Jesus' body, respectfully wraps it in clean linen, and buries it in his own new tomb sealed with a large rock. Again, two women observe the event as witnesses. Sometimes disciples appear unexpectedly "out of the woodwork." Even a simple but tender gesture such as this gives due honor to the Lord. Discipleship may be risky, but sometimes we can be surprised by those who suddenly step forward. Matthew also tells how the Jewish leaders petition Pilate to guard the tomb because of Jesus' teaching about the resurrection. They fear that his disciples will steal the body and claim a resurrection. Ironically, they claim that this would compound Jesus' alleged duplicity, when it is they who hypocritically have compounded deception upon deception in their opposition. Jesus' earlier words about "this evil generation" come to mind. Their final "imposture" truly becomes worse than before (v. 64; cf. 12:45). They try futilely to dominate Jesus in death as they had tried feebly to do so in his life. This is tantamount to saying that evil has a way of piling up exponentially if we allow it. Pilate, continuing his role of less than enthusiastic supporter of their plans, tells them to use their own resources and "secure it as best you can" (v. 65). Their actions of sealing the tomb and setting the guard show how fearful they are, but their attempts are futile in the face of God's power.

The Resurrection (28:1-15)

¹ After the sabbath, as the first day of the week was dawning, Mary Magdalene and the other Mary came to see the tomb. ² And behold, there was a great earthquake; for an angel of the Lord descended from heaven, approached, rolled back the stone, and sat upon it. ³ His appearance was like lightning and his clothing was white as snow. ⁴ The guards were shaken with fear of him and became like dead men. ⁵ Then the angel said to the women in reply, "Do not be afraid! I know that you are seeking Jesus the crucified. ⁶ He is not here, for he has been raised just as he said. Come and see the place where he lay. ⁷ Then go quickly and tell his disciples, 'He has been raised from the dead, and he is going before you to Galilee; there you will see him.' Behold, I have told you."

[8] Then they went away quickly from the tomb, fearful yet overjoyed, and ran to announce this to his disciples. [9] And behold, Jesus met them on their way and greeted them. They approached, embraced his feet, and did him homage. [10] Then Jesus said to them, "Do not be afraid. Go tell my brothers to go to Galilee, and there they will see me." [11] While they were going, some of the guards went into the city and told the chief priests all that had happened. [12] They assembled with the elders and took counsel; then they gave a large sum of money to the soldiers, [13] telling them, "You are to say, 'His disciples came by night and stole him while we were asleep.' [14] And if this gets to the ears of the governor, we will satisfy [him] and keep you out of trouble." [15] The soldiers took the money and did as they were instructed. And this story has circulated among the Jews to the present [day].

The final chapter of the Gospel consists of three terse scenes, the resurrection (28:1-10), the testimony of the guards (28:11-15), and the great commission (28:16-20). Two of the faithful women who had earlier been referenced go to the tomb on the day after the Sabbath, the first day of the week in the Jewish calendar, to "see" the tomb. As Matthew had noted during several significant events in Jesus' life, an earthquake occurs—a sign that God's power is at work. An angel in dazzling apparel approaches and rolls back the stone of the tomb. Paradoxically, this angelic being who has come to announce the resurrection causes the guards to become like dead men, paralyzed with fear. To the women, however, the angel exhorts them not to be afraid because Jesus has been raised as he foretold and is proceeding to Galilee. The tomb is empty, and they are to announce their message quickly. Galilee is where Jesus' ministry had begun. It is also the region identified with the Gentiles (4:15), symbolic of the worldwide mission to which Jesus will soon commission his disciples. On their way to announce this good news to the disciples, Jesus appears to them in a scene unique to Matthew's Gospel. They appropriately bow down in homage (*proskyneo*; 2:11; 14:33). Jesus repeats the message of the angel not to be afraid. They are, rather, to tell Jesus' companions that they will see him in Galilee.

Matthew's Spartan account of the resurrection masks its significance. Only by virtue of the resurrection does Jesus' message achieve its fullest stature. It announces God's victory; it vindicates Jesus' identity. This action of God that conquers the most ultimate of human experiences promises a future where, from the strictly human perspective, none can be expected. All of Jesus' teachings throughout the Gospel about heavenly reward and eternal life now reach a new level of realization. Jesus' resurrection validates his messianic identity and paradoxically confirms the fear of his opponents in the preceding scene (27:64). It also provides evidence that the sacrifices made for the sake of God's kingdom will be rewarded. Jesus' words are not empty promises but full of hope, and our faith is not in an empty tomb but in a crucified and risen Lord who can be encountered and worshiped in his abiding presence.

The women provide an accurate and reliable account of the events because they have consistently been present, from crucifixion to burial to resurrection. In contrast to their authentic witness the next scene relates the testimony of the guards who are bribed by the Jewish leaders to make up a story about the disciples stealing the body (vv. 11-15; cf. 27:64). Even after his death and resurrection, the leaders continue to plot against Jesus. They cannot let go, they cannot admit their failure. Their concocted tale confirms their anxiety. For Matthew, the story of the stolen body had currency among the Jews down to his own day (v. 15). The generic reference to "Jews" reflects the growing distance between Matthew's community and Judaism. The tale, in fact, was used at times against the early Christians to explain away the empty tomb. But Matthew's faith is not in an empty tomb per se but in a Risen Jesus. The false testimony of the guards stands in stark contrast to the authentic witness of the women.

The Great Commission (28:16-20)

[16]The eleven disciples went to Galilee, to the mountain to which Jesus had ordered them. [17]When they saw him, they worshiped, but they doubted. [18]Then Jesus approached and said to them, "All power in heaven and on earth has been given to me. [19]Go, therefore, and make disciples of all nations, baptizing them in the name of the Father, and of the Son, and of the Holy Spirit, [20]teaching them to observe all that I have commanded you. And behold, I am with you always, until the end of the age."

The final scene concludes the chapter and climaxes the whole Gospel. The great commission to the remaining eleven disciples takes place on the mountain in Galilee where Jesus had instructed them to go (vv. 16-20). Jesus had taught the disciples on a mountain, showed them a glimpse of glory on a mountain, had healed on a mountain, and now commissions them on a mountain. Their reaction to his approach is one of a combination of faith and doubt. The text is usually translated that they worshiped him but "some doubted," but the NAB's translation ("they worshiped, but they doubted") may reflect more accurately what is meant. Although the disciples have believed in Jesus throughout the Gospel, their faith has not been perfect. Remember that they were consistently chastised as those of "little faith" (6:30; 8:26; 14:31; 16:8). I think the present text reminds us that faith is seldom such a rock-solid reality that it is not accompanied, at least at times, by doubt when confronting challenges. Doubts and questions are not the enemy of faith; fear is. Thus the injunction against fear (28:5,10; cf. 14:27). So perhaps within individual disciples there were traces of doubt even as they believed in and worshiped the Risen Lord. Doubt can coexist with faith without destroying it.

Whereas he had earlier instructed them to preach and to heal, now their mission includes the command to *teach* all that Jesus had commanded. Matthew emphasizes the expansive nature of this scene by the fourfold use of the little word "all"

(all power, all nations, all Jesus taught, all days [NAB "always"]). Jesus has full authority from his Father to commission them, and they are told primarily to make disciples of all nations. They are to baptize in the name of the Trinity, to teach Jesus' teaching, and to trust that Jesus will abide with them even to the end of the ages. The Gospel has thus come full circle. Emmanuel, God-with-us, is present as Risen Lord and will accompany the disciples on their worldwide mission to spread the gospel. The mention of baptizing in the name of the Father, the Son and the Holy Spirit is unusual in the NT. We take this baptismal formula for granted. However, only much later, after the NT period, did Christians come to realize the significance of the nature of the Trinity as three persons in one God. While this exact understanding is unlikely in the time of Matthew, the Matthean community nevertheless must have practiced baptism by this liturgical formula, in contrast to the simpler formulae found elsewhere in the NT (cf. Acts 2:38; 8:16; Rom 6:3; Gal 3:27). The closest related formula is found in an early Christian document called the Didache (cf. Did 7:1). Thus, at least two early Christian documents provide testimony about the early development of such a baptismal formula. The seeds of later Christian insight about the nature of one God in three persons were planted very early.

The effect of this climactic scene is to call all disciples to evangelize, to give testimony to their faith, and to spread the Good News. This is where Matthew's favorite themes of Christology and ecclesiology flow seamlessly together. The Risen Christ in all his glory and his power commands the disciples to do what the Church does—spread the faith. As we attempt to fulfill Jesus' mission, we are assured that our efforts will not be alone. The Risen Lord will accompany us and abide with us, even to the end of the ages.

VII
Postscript

We have now finished a brief, spiritual reading of the Gospel of Matthew. We have merely scratched the surface of the text. Further reflection can lead to deeper insights, and more study can lead to deeper faith. I hope that the commentary has enticed you to want to study this Gospel in more detail. Each time the liturgical year of Matthew comes up in the liturgical cycle, we have a new opportunity to explore the Gospel again. To assist with further study, I recommend a few resources in the next section that could prove helpful. Remember, however, that nothing transcends the reading of the biblical text itself. As you progress in your own understanding of this intriguing Gospel, I pray that you will receive the grace of the good householder who takes from his storeroom new and old insights (13:52). Then you will have entered afresh the magical Matthean world of "the gospel of the kingdom."

For Further Study

Commentaries

Garland, David E. *Reading Matthew: A Literary and Theological Commentary on the First Gospel* (New York: Crossroad, 1993).

Hagner, Donald A. *Matthew 1–13* and *Matthew 14–28* in the *Word Biblical Commentary 33A and 33B* (Dallas: Word Books, 1993, 1995).

Hare, Douglas R. *Matthew* (Louisville: John Knox, 1993).

Harrington, Daniel J. *The Gospel of Matthew* (Collegeville: Liturgical Press, 1991).

Leske, Adrian. "Matthew," in *The International Bible Commentary* (Collegeville: Liturgical Press, 1998), 1253-1330.

Senior, Donald. *Matthew* (Nashville: Abingdon, 1997).

General Works

Brown, Raymond, E. "The Gospel according to Matthew," in *An Introduction to the New Testament* (New York: Doubleday, 1997), 171-224.

Carter, Warren. *Matthew: Storyteller, Interpreter, Evangelist* (Peabody, MA: Hendrickson, 1996).

Carter, Warren and John Paul Heil, *Matthew's Parables: Audience-Oriented Perspectives* (Washington, DC: Catholic Biblical Association, 1998).

Kingsbury, Jack Dean. *Matthew as Story* (2d ed., Philadelphia: Fortress, 1988).

———. *Matthew* (Nappanee, IN: Evangel Publishing, 1998).

Luz, Ulrich. *The Theology of the Gospel of Matthew* (Cambridge: Cambridge University, 1993).

Meier, John P. *The Vision of Matthew* (New York: Crossroad, 1991; originally 1979).

Powell, Mark Allen. *God With Us: A Pastoral Theology of Matthew's Gospel* (Minneapolis: Fortress, 1995).

Senior, Donald. *The Gospel of Matthew* (Nashville: Abingdon, 1997).

———. *What are they saying about Matthew?* (rev. ed.; New York: Paulist, 1996).

Stanton, Graham, N. *A Gospel for a New People: Studies in Matthew* (Edinburgh: T & T Clark, 1992).

In the Same Series from New City Press

Mark
From Death to Life
Dennis Sweetland
ISBN 1-56548-117-8, paper, 5 3/8 x 8 1/2, 216 pp.

Romans
The Good News According to Paul
Daniel Harrington
ISBN 1-56548-096-1, paper, 5 3/8 x 8 1/2, 152 pp.

First Corinthians
Building Up the Church
Vincent P. Branick
ISBN 1-56548-162-3, paper, 5 3/8 x 8 1/2, 152 pp.

Paul's Prison Letters
Scriptural Commentaries on Paul's Letters to Philemon,
the Philippians, and the Colossians
Daniel Harrington
ISBN 1-56548-088-0, paper, 5 3/8 x 8 1/2, 136 pp.

Revelation
The Book of the Risen Christ
Daniel Harrington
ISBN 1-56548-121-6, paper, 5 3/8 x 8 1/2, 168 pp.

To Order Phone 1-800-462-5980
www.newcitypress.com

In the Same Series from New City Press

Daniel
A Book for Troubling Times
Alexander A. Di Lella
ISBN 1-56548-087-2, paper, 5 3/8 x 8 1/2, 232 pp.

Song of Songs
The Love Poetry of Scripture
Dianne Bergant
ISBN 1-56548-100-3, paper, 5 3/8 x 8 1/2, 168 pp.

Other Biblical Readings from New City Press

How To Read the Gospels
Answers to Common Questions
Daniel J. Harrington
ISBN 1-56548-076-7, paper, 5 1/8 x 8, 96 pp.

* * *

Call to the Center
The Gospel's Invitation to Deeper Prayer
Basil Pennington
ISBN 1-56548-070-8, paper, 5 3/8 x 8 1/2, 168 pp.

To Order Phone 1-800-462-5980
www.newcitypress.com